Young Writers 200[...]

PLAYGRO[...]

Let your cre[...]ivity flow...

ode
limerick / haiku
rhyme
ball[...]

my poems

- Inspirations From
The West Midlands
Edited by Steve Twelvetree

 Young**Writers**

First published in Great Britain in 2005 by:
Young Writers
Remus House
Coltsfoot Drive
Peterborough
PE2 9JX
Telephone: 01733 890066
Website: www.youngwriters.co.uk

SB ISBN 1 84602 224 X

Foreword

Young Writers was established in 1991 and has been passionately devoted to the promotion of reading and writing in children and young adults ever since. The quest continues today. Young Writers remains as committed to the fostering of burgeoning poetic and literary talent as ever.

This year's Young Writers competition has proven as vibrant and dynamic as ever and we are delighted to present a showcase of the best poetry from across the UK. Each poem has been carefully selected from a wealth of *Playground Poets* entries before ultimately being published in this, our thirteenth primary school poetry series.

Once again, we have been supremely impressed by the overall high quality of the entries we have received. The imagination, energy and creativity which has gone into each young writer's entry made choosing the best poems a challenging and often difficult but ultimately hugely rewarding task - the general high standard of the work submitted amply vindicating this opportunity to bring their poetry to a larger appreciative audience.

We sincerely hope you are pleased with our final selection and that you will enjoy *Playground Poets - Inspirations From The West Midlands* for many years to come.

Contents

Delves Junior School

Jabir Uddin (7)	13
Samuel Greenhough (7)	13
Abbey Thompson (8)	14
Connern Gilbert (8)	14
Jaskiran Nagra (8)	15
Rosie Evans (8)	15
Isha Khan (8)	16
Kye Grundy (7)	16
Iqra Atiq (8)	17
Cody Whitney (8)	17
Halina Hayre (7)	18
Vikash Patel (7)	18
Chloe Webster (8)	19
Jodie Fisher (8)	19
George Cartlidge (8)	20
Aekam Bains (7)	20
Charlotte Farmer (7)	21
Wasif Ahmed (8)	21
Daniel Bird (8)	22
Karisha Edie (8)	22
Naomi Bingham (8)	23
Conor Ford (7)	23
Jeena Patel (8)	24
Lauryn Morgan (7)	24
Nikhel Chhiba (8)	25
Zoë Pearce (7)	25
Matthew Guy (8)	26
Sam Bradley (8)	26
Tim Sheward (7)	27
April Lunn (8)	28
Luke Taylor-Warner (8)	28
Daveena Kataria (8)	29
Danielle Camm (8)	29
Michael Edwards (8)	30
Gurvinder Bhangal (8)	30
Joseph Slater (9)	31
Craig Sillifant (8)	31
Shane Akbar (7)	32
Zennah Hall (8)	32

Dingle Primary School

Tammy Poole (11)	32
Joe Haden (11)	33
Sophia Dimopoulou (11)	33
Emily Fisher (11)	34
Chloe Rutherford (11)	34
Abigail Holloway (10)	35
Daniel Fellows (11)	35
Daniel Lamb (11)	36
Christopher Round (11)	36
Ben Jones (11)	37
Thomas Bowen (11)	38
Hayley Siviter (11)	38
Martin Siviter (11)	39
Stefanie Ward (10)	40
Chloe Gillard (11)	40
Rachel Wood (11)	41

Eversfield Preparatory School

Jacob Small (9)	41
Robert Woolley (8)	41
Tom Lilburn (11)	42
Alastair Harryman (9)	42
Jessica Wevill (8)	42
Bhavik Parmar (11)	43
Christopher Beaumont-Dark (9)	44
Sunil Sidhu (10)	44
John Grimme (8)	45
Jordan Knight (8)	45
Jonathan Oliver (8)	45
Daniel Oliver (10)	46
Ashkaan Golestani (10)	46
Joseph Jones (9)	47
Bronte Armstrong (8)	47
Ryan Dhadwal (9)	47
Keelan Fadden-Hopper (9)	48
Charlotte Wilson (9)	48
Sophie Hill (8)	48
Marco Consiglio (9)	49
Samantha Deakin (9)	49
Harvey Stevens (9)	49

Meghan Winter (9)   50
Ben Elkin (8)   50
Ben Thornley (9)   51

Glynne Primary School
Sophie Horne   51
Eve Mallen (9)   52
Nathan Jones (9)   52
Bethanie Lowe (9)   53
Ben Millett-Kirkham (8)   53
Eleanor Jordan (9)   54
Adam Brown (9)   54
Andrew Meese (9)   55
Russell Homer (9)   55
Tom Aston (9)   55
Isobel Beech (9)   56
Joe Sherwood (9)   56
Molly Bowater   57
Alex Spittle (9)   57
Scott Badger (9)   58
Michael Saxon (9)   58
Daniel Evans (8)   59

Great Bridge Primary School
Ryan Cox (9)   59
Samantha Hubbard (10)   60
Aaron Moore (10)   61
Luke Hosell (9)   61
Abigail Golding (11)   62
Brandon Wright (11)   62
Sundeep Thandi (11)   63
Suhail Perager (9)   63
Ajay Singh (11)   64
Awais Younis (10)   64
Samantha Oakley (11)   65
Stacey Nock (10)   65
Sarah Hampson (10)   66
Chloe Hadley (10)   66
Charlotte Cox (10)   67
Rebecca Hughes (10)   67
Natalie Oakes (10)   69

Lindens Primary School

Heidi McManus (11)	69
Toni Stevens (11)	70
Samuel Crawford (11)	70
Kiran Gill (11)	71
Amber Robinson (10)	71
Shanice Prince (11)	72
Katie Perkins (11)	72
Sophie Fisher (10)	73
Josh Finegan (11)	73
Jade Morris (10)	73
Laura Murphy (11)	74
Catherine Ball (11)	74
Richard Wheeler (11)	75
Ben Whatley (11)	75
Jozef Doyle (11)	76
Megan Saul (11)	76
Shiv Parekh (11)	76
Oliver Willis (10)	77

Little Heath Primary School

Sukhpreet Nainu (9)	77
Elisha Jawaid (9)	78
Karenjit Kaur Somal (8)	78

Little Sutton Primary School

Nina Kapur (10)	79
Samantha Hobbs (11)	80
Madison Millward-Murray (11)	80
Alexandra Paxton (11)	81
Borbala Balint (11)	81
Arjun Singh Mann (11)	82
Fiona Rollings (11)	83
Jemma Westgate (11)	83
Chloe O'Carroll (11)	84
Eleanor Biggs (10)	84
Richard Robinson (11)	85
Andrew Tsiappourdhi (10)	85
Joanna Errington (11)	86
Ben Griffiths (10)	87
Brogan Hadland (11)	88

Bethany Davis-Jones (11)	88
Ellie Iezekiel (10)	89
Abbie Dosell (11)	89
Emma Hall (10)	90
Abigail Holt (10)	91
Keeley Smith (10)	92
Alice Veitch (11)	93
Suzanne Everett (11)	94
Harmeet Chatha (11)	94
Deborah Pryor (10)	95
Amelia Tipper (10)	96
Alex Nash (10)	97
Aaron Bagga (11)	97
Rebecca Jarvis (10)	98
Daniel Karandikar (10)	99
Harvey George (10)	100
Marcos Padilla (10)	101
Anisha Bagga (10)	102
Sarah Kelly (10)	103
Hayley Chapman (10)	104
Andrew Smith (10)	105
Kimberly Brown (11)	106
Caroline Jeffery (10)	107
Jonathan Lane (10)	108
Josie Rea-Miotto (10)	109
Jessica Nutt (11)	110
George Lakey (11)	110
Grace Chapman (11)	111
Raenia Soyannwo (11)	111
Guy Rogers (11)	112
James Huskisson (11)	113
Martyn Ludlow (9)	114
Julia Barbour (10)	115
Marcus Rowbotham (11)	116
Jessica Hipkiss (11)	116
Natasha Cope (10)	117
Bethany Lea-Redmond (10)	118
Louka Nicodemou (10)	119
Becky Richards (10)	120
Gemma Shepherd (10)	121
William Banks (10)	122

Mount Pleasant Primary School

Todd Millward (11)	122
Ryan Fellows (9)	123
Bethany Wilkins (10)	123
Hayley Whyte (10)	123
Bethany Smith (10)	124
Gemma Raybould (10)	124
Sam Freestone (10)	125
Anthony Thomas (11)	125
Katie-Jo Clarke (10)	126
Sophie Round (7)	126
Matthew Round (10)	127
Matthew Simmonds (10)	128
Adam Lambe (9)	128
Katie North (11)	129
Charlie Heaton (9)	129
Georgia Williams (11)	130
Leah Bangham (10)	130
Georgia Fitzsimmons (7)	131
Jack Brookes (10)	131
Tiffany Johnstone (10)	132
Daniel Pearson (9)	132
Ella Morgan (7)	133
Abigail Homer (8)	134
Reece Bourne (8)	135
Jack Green (10)	135
Adam Lowe (8)	136
Scott Smith (8)	136
Lucy Baker (7)	136
Jordan Debra-Washington (10)	137
Danielle Baker (10)	137
Andrew Raybould (9)	137
Aaran Tranter (9)	138
Rio Wood (10)	138
Matthew Jones (10)	139
Laura Whitehead (9)	139
Emily Leipacher (7)	139
Daniel Layland (9)	140
Melvyn Mathews (9)	140
Olivia Fullwood (10)	140
Victoria Webb (10)	141
Sandeep Patel (9)	141

James Hampson (6)	141
Lucy Bradley (8)	142
Daniel Woodfield (10)	142
Louisa Hampson (9)	143
Estelle Pedley (7)	143
Chandler Massey (7)	143
Thomas Taylor (9)	144
Nathan Greenwood (8)	144
Bradley Saunders (10)	145
Ellouise Banks (8)	145
Bethany Madkins (11)	146
Brandan Slater (10)	147
Rebecca Bradley (7)	147
Daniel Appleton (10)	148
Abby Byrne (8)	148
Katie Whitehead (7)	149
Rikesh Patel (10)	149
Daniel Turley (8)	150
Rory King (7)	150
Alex Sambidge (8)	151

New Oscott Junior School

Ameera Moore (8)	151
Emma Jeeves (8)	151
Ryan Ledward (8)	152

Rough Hay Primary School

Rebecca Booth (10)	152
Chloè Richards (11)	153
Brandon Maxfield (11)	153
Joseph Evans (11)	154
Beau Westwood (10)	154
Michael Collins (10)	155
Katie Griffiths (10)	155
Jessica Saunders (11)	156
Jade Webb (11)	156
Stephanie Eccleston (11)	157
Matthew Bott (11)	157
Victoria Greenway-Brown (11)	158
Joshua Talbot (11)	158
Kyle Smart (11)	159

The Poems

Fish On A Plate

I'm a piece of fish on a plate,
And I'm about to know my fate.
I'm about to be spooned into a mouth,
I'm pretty sure I'm heading south.

Some sharp teeth are biting me,
I want them to go desperately.
All squashed I land on a tongue,
If I look down I can see their lung.

Next I'm in the gullet, down I float,
I can see the stomach; it's warm like a coat.
In I go, in my place,
Now I'm in the digestive juice race.

I spin and bounce, like a ball,
I break into pieces that are very small.
The water has now been sucked from me,
Now I'm as solid as can be.

Next I go to the small intestine,
I get really small and I'm very keen.
It's nearly the end now,
I'm waiting *'Oh wow!'*

I see a toilet a bit like a dish,
It's waiting for my undigested fish.
So my journey is certainly complete,
What an amazing, marvellous feat!

Cathy Cook (10)

Annoying Little Sisters

They stomp up the stairs
And demolish your bed,
And before you know it
You're seeing red!

You shout down the stairs
And Mum comes to help,
Your little sister kicks you
You start to yelp!

Dad comes home, he's in a bad mood
When he enters the kitchen
He demands 'Where's my food?'

My sister says so sweetly
She really is a cheat,
'It's not quite ready Daddy
But please give me a sweet.'

If she gets into trouble
Beware: she blames it on you,
Your mum and dad will believe her,
They will say, 'Get to your room!'

Most sisters use up all your make-up
When they've finished putting it on
They look like a cuthabluraplopup!

So now you know all about
The evil side of *her,*
Yes, I mean little sisters
They're just as bad as they always were!

Laura Harris (10)
Albrighton Junior School

Deep Blue Sea

The ocean floor is deep and dark,
This is where you'll find a hungry shark.

Coral reefs more than one hundred feet deep
Fishes living in the deep, blue sea.

Cocktails, eels, cod, haddock, sardines
Don't forget the octopus.

Little fish with shining scales,
Fleeing from alarming whales.

A lake's too small for a whale to roam,
That's why it calls the sea its home.

Little starfish goes on dancing
Even with a shark advancing.

The oyster has a gift to hide,
A priceless pearl grows deep inside.

Ashley Hilson (9)
Albrighton Junior School

My Horse

This is a rap about my horse,
She's a great runner around the course,
Her coat is white,
She's such a sight,
She had to finish the line
And she looked fine,
And when she finished, I shouted, 'She's mine!'
Confident in every stride,
She looks the brightest with pride.

Hannah Logan (10)
Albrighton Junior School

Mr Hulme's Leaving Poem

The word went out across the land
That Mr Hulme was leaving his happy band.

'Oh dear what a shock!' said Mrs Jones
In her posh frock.
Mr Jones was all a quiver
When he found out he jumped in the river.

Maximum mouse will be no more as
Mr Hulme is taking him on tour.
We're going to miss you an awful lot
When you go on holiday, let's hope it's hot!

So pack your pencils, rulers and rubber,
Off you go helping others.
Enjoy your trip wherever you go,
We'll always remember you're our star of the show!

Rebecca Ellsey (10)
Albrighton Junior School

Sadness Poem

My hair shall not glow until my troubles are sorted,
My forehead is full of melancholy,
My brows are low with sadness,
My ears wilt with misery.

My lashes are heavy with misery, sorrow, guilt and mourning,
My pupils are big with sorrow,
My eyes are a bag of flowing tears,
My nose droops down with disappointment.

My cheeks sag low with troubles,
My lips tremble with fear and guilt,
My chin is grim.
I shouldn't have done it!

Emma Boden (10)
Albrighton Junior School

Guess

In the amberness of the evening,
The gentle swish-swishing noise keeps me awake.
It is a lovely sound.
I'd quite like to lie here and listen.
I reach to the window and open it.
So blue, so beautiful, so good.
I clamber back into bed.
Soon I am asleep.
I am dreaming.

Georgia Potts (8)
Albrighton Junior School

Guess

It leaps like a roadrunner.
It camouflages in long grass.
It lives in the tropics.
It nips with its dreaded claws.
It's multicoloured browns and light yellows.
It runs like an elegant athlete.
It eats new plants and tasty meat.
Its teeth are as sharp as knives.

Aaron Marsh (9)
Albrighton Junior School

Guess

They are smart,
They look like devils,
They shoot like a falcon,
They don't linger
They hunt like a tiger
They work like an army
They fight like a lion.

Victor Ingham (8)
Albrighton Junior School

Kite

The
Ruby red
Kite is flying
High in the sky.
Passes the clouds
Passing by. It shines
In the sun, flying
High, low, round
And round.
Look up
You
Will
See
A
Shape
And
The
Kite
The
Children
Hold
The
Wiggly
String.

Olivia Spencer (8)
Albrighton Junior School

Guess The Subject

It spits like a sports car going too fast.
It is hot like an oven.
It's yellow, red and orange.
If it burns you it will hurt like a bee sting.
It loves coal.
Answer: Fire.

Beth Martin (8)
Albrighton Junior School

My Friend

This is a poem about my friend,
This is how it might just end.
I said I would send him a gorgeous girl,
One to treasure for all the world.

Michael Grubb (9)
Albrighton Junior School

My Name Is Jodie

My name is Jodie but call me Jo.
At home my dad thinks I'm the star of the show.
My mum is busy most of the time.
So my job is to keep them all in line.

Jodie Yewbrey (10)
Albrighton Junior School

Sports Day

Sports day is the best
A lot better than the rest
We play it on the playground field
Although our lips are never sealed!

Shouting, screaming all the time
Willing our team to cross the line
If they lose we'll try again
Then we'll have a race for men.

Sports day is the best
A lot better than the rest
Than the games we play in school
Anyone can play these games, anyone at all.

Georgia Chaunkria (9)
Birchills CE School

There's A Well In . . .

There's a well in the playground
Let's all take a look
Someone's fell down, she was reading a book
The fire engines come now
To pull her back up
But what is that noise?
The teacher's shouting
And all I can hear is . . .
Fight, fight, fight!
The bell is ringing and
Now it is quiet!

Paige Clegg (9)
Birchills CE School

The Snail

It has . . .
A head like squidgy cotton wool
Tentacles like squelchy lollipop sticks
A shell like a wooden spiral shape
A body like a slimy hosepipe
Leaves a trail like sticky orange sauce.

Kieran Brazier (9)
Colley Lane Primary School

There Was A Young Boy From Crewe

There was a young boy from Crewe
Who went to a really good zoo
He saw a monkey
Who was a bit chunky
And he wore an enormous shoe.

Alex Massey (8)
Colley Lane Primary School

Months Of The Year

January is the start of the year
And we walk down the pier.
February is so much fun
I always have a tasty bun.
March is the beginning of spring
And we all start to sing.
April is when the flowers grow
They're so pretty I do know!
May, oh I love May
Because it is my birthday.
June is also nice
It lets me play with my dice.
July is so hot
I start thinking I'm about to rot.
August is when harvest starts
Lots of people are playing darts.
September is so fine
Sportsmen run across the line.
October is so great
The fishermen collect their bait.
November is so boring
Most animals start snoring.
December is so cold
Lots more blankets are then sold.

Jacob Wilkes (9)
Colley Lane Primary School

Owen's Limerick

There was a boy called Owen
Who didn't know where he was goin'
He went to the shop
To buy a bottle of pop
But ended up in Halesowen!

Owen Charles (9)
Colley Lane Primary School

Winnie The Witch

W ebs of spiders hang around her house.
I cicles are horrible to Winnie.
N ever ask Winnie for spells, they always go wrong.
N obody knows that Winnie's a witch.
I n Winnie's house everything is black.
E ven the cat is sick of Winnie.

T hen she waves her wand . . . 'Abracadabra'
H elicopters, cars, planes, she crashes into everything.
E verybody hates it when she waves her wand.

W e all think she's weird.
I sn't she cool?
T he world's greatest
C lap for Winnie.
H ooray, hooray, hooray!

Jessica Smith (9)
Colley Lane Primary School

Birthday

B ikes, scooter, everything you could wish for.
I ce cream sundaes and jelly too.
R eal puppies just for you.
T wister the game and many more.
H ide-and-seek, wonder where they're hiding?
D ogs bark at the next-door neighbours.
A pple pie and pizza too.
Y ahoo, my birthday is here.

Lauren Blake (9)
Colley Lane Primary School

The Football Man

There's a man I know who roams the land
With a bright red football in his hand!
He kicks it here, he kicks it there
He kicks that football everywhere!
He throws it up, he throws it down
He throws it all around the town.
He kicks his football low and high
Until it nearly hits the sky
He bounces it round his head
He even kicks it in his bed
And when he slides beneath the sheets
He even kicks it in his sleep.

Sara Uddin (9)
Colley Lane Primary School

There Was A Young Boy From Crewe

There was a young boy from Crewe
Who wore an enormous shoe
He saw a clown
Who went down town
Whatever could he do?

Jake Althorp (9)
Colley Lane Primary School

The Queen's Last Day

There was a young boy from Marston Green
Who liked to watch Mr Bean
He thought he could fly
But he fell from the sky
And landed on the Queen.

Adam Totten (9)
Colley Lane Primary School

There Was A Young Boy Named Dwayne

There was a young boy named Dwayne,
Who definitely had no brain,
He walked into a wall,
And fell into a pool,
I'm ashamed that he lives down my lane.

Bethan Davis (9)
Colley Lane Primary School

Drama Queen

There was a young girl called Laura
Acting was the only job for her
From the age of sixteen
She'll be a drama queen
'Cause everything else did bore her.

Laura Alston (9)
Colley Lane Primary School

Spain Limerick

There once was a girl called Jayne
Who flew round the world by plane
Through rain and sun
She had such fun
But her favourite place was Spain.

Emily Foley (8)
Colley Lane Primary School

A Horrifying Limerick

I was on duty in the guardroom
When a zombie arrived from Khartoum
So I squirted shampoo
And swore in Hindu
And today he is back in his tomb.

Abbie Cooper
Colley Lane Primary School

Sunflowers

S ome flowers are spiky
U nder the sunflower there is a root
N otice the sunflowers in the sun
F lowers are beautiful
L ong sunflowers grow in soil
O ften they grow with water and soil
W ater the sunflowers every day
E very sunflower looks the same
R ain is good for sunflowers.

Jabir Uddin (7)
Delves Junior School

Sunflowers

S waying gently in the sun
U sing water and sun to make sunflowers
N ow the flowers are dancing in the breeze
F alling on the ground
L ots of petals flying in the air
O range sunflowers flying and crackling
W ith lots of petals
E verywhere is lovely
R oses and sunflowers make a big dragon.

Samuel Greenhough (7)
Delves Junior School

Sunflowers

S waying smoothly through the fields
U nder the breeze the sunflowers sway
N eck to neck blow together
F lapping their petals everywhere
L ying in the field
O h! Roots grow under the sunflowers
W ind slows the sunflowers side to side
E verywhere in fields you might see sunflowers
R oots live under the plants.

Abbey Thompson (8)
Delves Junior School

Sunflowers

S hiny sunflowers swaying in the morning breeze
U nder the bright morning sky
N ice shining sun
F at sunflower heads
L ight not heavy
O utside sunflower seeds are dropped
W ide but also thin
E ven kings grow them
R ainy days sunflowers grow.

Connern Gilbert (8)
Delves Junior School

Sunflowers

S unflowers standing tall
U nder the bright blue sky
N ice sunflowers swaying by the fresh trees
F alling raindrops helping the sunflowers grow
L ightning in the dark getting very scared
O h! What lovely sunflowers
W indows you can see out, it is a sunflower!
E very sunflower is beautiful
R eally happy and dreaming of the beautiful sunflowers! *Zzzz*

Jaskiran Nagra (8)
Delves Junior School

Sunflowers

S miling sunflowers standing tall
U p where the sun is they stare and stare
N ice pretty flowers swaying in the breeze
F aces smiling up at you
L ovely smooth yellow petals
O ver the fields they are spread beautiful, yellow, glistening
W e all think sunflowers are pretty
E njoy the sun oh pretty sunflowers
R ise to the sky sunflowers and touch the sun.

Rosie Evans (8)
Delves Junior School

Sunflowers

S unflowers standing tall
U nder the bright blue sky
N ever go black or white
F ound a sunflower that is bright
L eaves rough and hairy
O h! Please don't pick them or they will die
W ater every day then they will grow
E very sunflower is yellow
R ain waters the sunflowers.

Isha Khan (8)
Delves Junior School

Sunflowers

S unflowers standing tall
U nder the bright blue sky
N ice rabbits sitting by the sun
F lowers are nice
L eaving flowers behind in the house
O h what fun by the sun
W hat beautiful flowers
E verywhere I go flowers grow
R ough sunflowers standing tall.

Kye Grundy (7)
Delves Junior School

Sunflowers

S unflower standing tall
U nder the bright blue sky
N ice rough leaves
F lowers are bright
L iving flowers
O h what are you doing?
W et flowers
E very day I watch the flowers grow
R ain is good.

Iqra Atiq (8)
Delves Junior School

Sunflowers

S unflowers sitting still
U nder the blue shiny sky
N ight is light and bright
F lowers are bright
L ight sunflowers are bright
O h! Sunflowers are bright
W e like sunflowers when they are bright
E veryone likes sunflowers
R ight away they sway lightly.

Cody Whitney (8)
Delves Junior School

Sunflowers

S unflowers standing tall
U nlike any flowers
N ight comes
F lowers are nice and beautiful
L ight flowers standing tall
O ther flowers are not as nice
W here sunflowers are beautiful
E ven sunflowers smell nice
R ain falls on them but they don't care!

Halina Hayre (7)
Delves Junior School

Sunflowers

S unflowers standing tall
U nusual faces staring at us
N ice, sparkly and tall
F anning the ground
L ower than the sun
O h! Look how they sway in the wind
W ith the other flowers
E ven taller than bluebells
R iding with the wind.

Vikash Patel (7)
Delves Junior School

Sunflowers

S unflowers standing tall
U nder the bright blue sky
N ever that harmful to the others around
F lowers that sway are the flowers today
L ovely, yes they are lovely
O h yes in the breeze they wave their leaves
W aving at them is so much fun
E veryone wants to know why they sway
R ight away they can sway.

Chloe Webster (8)
Delves Junior School

Sunflower

S unflower waving in the wind
U nder the yellow, bright sun
N ever falling out of the ground
F lying up into the sky
L ike the trees around
O h! They grow up quickly
W hen I go and water them they are just so tall
E very sunflower has yellow sharp petals
R ain can make them grow.

Jodie Fisher (8)
Delves Junior School

Sunflower

S unny sunflowers standing in the breeze
U nder the bright blue sky
N ice shining sun forever be there
F or the sunflowers to live
L ovely, smooth, yellow petals
O h! Why do you fall off?
W hy do your seeds fall as well?
E asy to love you oh sunflowers
R adiant and beautiful are the sunflowers.

George Cartlidge (8)
Delves Junior School

Sunflowers

S unflowers standing brightly tall
U nder the bright sunny sky
N ever rolling down the hill
F alling raindrops giving water
L eaves dropping off the plants
O h! They do grow quickly
W henever the sun is out it grows really, really tall
E very sunflower is really jolly
R eally! Sunflowers do grow.

Aekam Bains (7)
Delves Junior School

Sunflowers

S unflowers standing tall and straight
U nder the sun proud and strong
N ice bright flowers
F unny little plants swaying from side to side
L ying by flowers having fun
O h! What fun by the sun
W hat beautiful flowers by the sun
E verywhere I go flowers grow
R eading about flowers all night long.

Charlotte Farmer (7)
Delves Junior School

Sunflowers

S unflowers standing tall
U nder the bright blue sky
N othing but beautiful
F lowers that face the sun
L onely till they reach the sky
O h! They move in the breeze
W hen the breeze is blowing
E vergreen leaves that are rough
R esting because fresh water from the rain hits the flowers.

Wasif Ahmed (8)
Delves Junior School

Sunflowers

S unflowers standing in a row
U nder the red sun
N ot under the rain
F alling rain helps it grow
L eaves are very rough
O h! What lovely flowers
W ater gives them health
E very sunflower is nice
R eal sunflowers grow.

Daniel Bird (8)
Delves Junior School

Sunflowers

S unflowers standing tall
U nder the bright blue sky
N ice and pretty
F lowers are pretty
L eaves are wonderful and pretty
O h!
W hat a wonderful bright sight
E very day I see them I think they are pretty
R eally pretty and wonderful.

Karisha Edie (8)
Delves Junior School

Sunflowers

S unflowers blowing in the wind
U nder the shiny bright sky
N othing but beautiful flowers
F lowers being blown by the wind
L oads of flowers on a big, big hill
O h! What beautiful bright flowers
W hen winds blow, flowers wave
E very flower is beautiful and bright
R eally some flowers are not as beautiful.

Naomi Bingham (8)
Delves Junior School

Sunflowers

S unflowers standing tall
U nusual little faces looking at me
N ice bright sunflowers
F unny little sunflowers bobbing about
L ovely little yellow heads
O h! What fun in the sun
W iggly sunflowers in the sun
E verywhere I go sunflowers keep on growing
R ising flowers up to the sun.

Conor Ford (7)
Delves Junior School

Sunflowers

S unflowers gleaming in the sun
U sing their might to grow tall
N ow they are tall, they might die
F loating in the warm breeze
L ittle sunflowers grow tall when the rain and the sun come
O h! We shouldn't step on our marvellous sunflowers
W ill they grow nice and tall?
E normous flowers can be used for sunflower oil
R ain might make them nice and bright.

Jeena Patel (8)
Delves Junior School

Sunflowers

S waying gently in the sun
U sing all of their might to grow really tall
N ow what will happen with my sunflower?
F lowers gleaming in the sun
L ovely bright yellow petals
O h! My sunflower has grown tall
W hat a very lovely sight
E normous flowers can be used for sunflower oil
R ain falling down to the sunflowers.

Lauryn Morgan (7)
Delves Junior School

Sunflowers

S unflowers, sunflowers what would we do without you?
U p, up grow, grow sunflowers, grow to Heaven
N obody can resist how popular you are
F ields are packed with you
L ovely children like to play hide-and-seek
O h! How tall can you get?
W hat will we do without your oil
E nemies are naughty
R are animals die! Flowers eventually die.

Nikhel Chhiba (8)
Delves Junior School

Sunflowers

S unflowers swaying in the gentle breeze
U p in the sky the rain falls down so the sunflowers can grow
N esting birds right up in the trees
F lowers floating right above the hard, rough ground
L ittle sunflowers growing from the ground
O pen little petals, open and grow
W rite to the sunflowers grow, grow, grow and see the world
   on the count of three
E ggs cracking right by me
R ise from the ground fast as can be.

Zoë Pearce (7)
Delves Junior School

Sunflowers

S unflower, sunflower rise up to the sun
U nder the ground are roots
N ever underestimate the power of rain
F ollow the sunflower, follow the sun!
L ook up to the sky
O il comes from sunflower seeds
W elcome to the sunflower
E veryone dance with the sunflowers
R oots are dying quickly.

Matthew Guy (8)
Delves Junior School

Sunflowers

S mooth sunflowers shining in the sun
U nder the sunflowers up tall in the grass
N ecks like a giraffe
F lowers as bright as the sun
L ooking up to the sky
O h, the grass staring at the sunflowers
W ater makes sunflowers grow
E nergy from the sun making the sunflowers grow
R ain and sun good for growing.

Sam Bradley (8)
Delves Junior School

Sunflowers

S waying gently in the sun
U nderneath there are big roots
N ice petals are falling down
F lowers gazing up at the sun
L ooking cheerful and bright
O h! The roots die, the flower dies
W ater makes the flower grow tall
E veryone smiles at the sunflowers
R ows of sunflowers in a hot summer.

Tim Sheward (7)
Delves Junior School

Sunflowers

S unflowers grow
U nder the sun
N ew flowers grow from seeds
F lowers need water
L ooking at the sun
O h! How beautiful
W aving flower in the garden
E njoy them before they die
R oots are important.

Thomas Perks (8)
Delves Junior School

Sunflowers

S ummer sun shines down on the sunflower
U nder the sunflower the roots are growing
N ew sunflowers growing
F aces looking up at the sky
L ight from the sun makes them grow
O h they're so beautiful
W here are they?
E very flower looks so pretty under the sun
R oots growing one by one.

April Lunn (8)
Delves Junior School

Sunflowers

S unflowers, fantastic and bright
U nder the ground sunflower seeds grow and grow
N ow what happens to the sunflowers?
F lowers sway in the breeze right and left
L ovely sunflowers yellow and brown
O h they are beautiful
W onderful flowers different colours
E verybody enjoys looking at sunflowers
R oots alive, flower alive.

Luke Taylor-Warner (8)
Delves Junior School

Sunflowers

S ummer sun breezing gently
U nderground roots appear
N ewly grown yellow petals fall
F unny fur seeds in the middle
L ooking like a lion at the sun
O verflowing water helping it to grow
W aving sunflowers swaying at the sun
E very one of them is sure to smile
R ows of flowers yellow and bright.

Daveena Kataria (8)
Delves Junior School

Sunflowers

S unflowers all standing in a row
U nder the dazzling sun
N early as tall as a tree
F urry and rough leaves
L ooking up to the sun
O n the swaying grass
W onderful faces and leaves
E verybody likes sunflowers
R oots die, sunflower dies.

Danielle Camm (8)
Delves Junior School

Sunflowers

S unlight and water making it grow
U niting the flowers all together
N ow the flowers are happier and growing more
F lowing about on the earth and the ground
L ooking like a lion, so fierce but really it's gentle
O h! How it looks beautiful and warm in your heart
W e should admire the beautiful sight of the sunflower
E very summer they grow taller and taller like us growing
R ain dropping all over the field which the sunflower lives in.

Michael Edwards (8)
Delves Junior School

Sunflowers

S unflowers wave in the light breeze
U nder the hot sunny sun
N umber of sunflowers standing in a row
F low and wave in the wind
L ion faces looking at you
O h! See how beautiful they are!
W aving side to side
E njoy playing with them before they die!
R ain gives food and drink.

Gurvinder Bhangal (8)
Delves Junior School

Sunflowers

S unflower swaying in the breeze
U nder roots growing in the ground
N ew flowers growing
F aces like lions on the flowers
L ight sun beaming on the flowers
O ur world loves sunflowers
W eeds in the ground growing like fingers
E very flower looks pretty
R oots die, flowers die.

Joseph Slater (9)
Delves Junior School

Sunflowers

S unflowers waving in the breeze
U gly looking when they die
N ow what does the flower do?
F ace looks like a lion
L ooking at the sun
O range and brown seeds in the middle
W ater will make it survive
E ats soil from the ground
R oots die . . . flower dies.

Craig Sillifant (8)
Delves Junior School

Sunflowers

S unny sunflowers waving in the wind
U nder the ground roots grow
N ew sunflowers grow in the summer
F inally the middle grows seeds
L ovely sunflowers grow
O h! Now the plants are all dead
W hat happens now?
E very sunflower is looking up at the sun
R oots are really important.

Shane Akbar (7)
Delves Junior School

Sunflowers

S unflower is so tall
U p, up to the sky
N ice pretty petals
F lowers are beautiful
L ong stems
O h look at them
W onderful in a vase
E very flower smells sweet
R eally tall flowers.

Zennah Hall (8)
Delves Junior School

The Castle

Through the castle,
There is some stairs,
Up the stairs there is a courtyard.
Through the courtyard there are more stairs
Up the stairs there is a young girl
Waiting for me
Just waiting . . .

Tammy Poole (11)
Dingle Primary School

My Dog

My dog is very cuddly
When I put my head to his chest
He's funny when he licks my ears
And he's better than the rest

I sleep with him in my mom's bed
He even crawls under the quilt
He doesn't eat any of his food
So I have to feed him myself

I once chased my dog around the house
And he knocked his water over
Next day my dad slipped over it
The hospital told him he'd broken his toe

But the best thing about my dog
Is that he's always there
He always keeps me company
And he likes to lick my hair.

Joe Haden (11)
Dingle Primary School

My Cousin Lewis

My cousin Lewis, he is great,
He has always been my best mate.

He is always there for me,
He never lets me down,
He reminds me of a circus clown.

He makes me laugh when I am sad,
Because he is crazy and mad.
But I mean it in a good way, not bad.

I think you've guessed it,
He is the best,
He is better than the rest.

Sophia Dimopoulou (11)
Dingle Primary School

The Dreaded Adventure Week

What's it going to be like?
What am I going to do?
I don't know but I know I'm very nervous.
The fencing,
What if I hurt myself?
Bridge building,
What happens if the bridge falls while I'm on it?
Abseiling,
What happens if I can't do it?
Will my friends laugh at me?
Rock climbing,
What if I fall?
Will my friends think I'm scared of doing stuff?
I have mixed feelings.
Will it be strange, will it be scary, will it be fun?
Will I miss my mom and dad?
I don't know but I'll find out soon!

Emily Fisher (11)
Dingle Primary School

My Mom

She is loving
She is loving and caring
She is loving, caring and understanding
She is loving, caring, understanding and friendly
She is loving, caring, understanding, friendly and forgiving
She is loving, caring, understanding, friendly, forgiving
and stands by me
She is my mom.

Chloe Rutherford (11)
Dingle Primary School

Pioneer Centre

Counting days to adventure fun,
Waiting for the time to come,
What might happen in two weeks time?

Swimming, climbing, staying up,
Abseiling by a click of a hook,
What might happen in one week's time?

Dive under covers,
Send the ghosts to their mothers,
What might happen in two days time?

Sneak out late at night,
Friends run away in fright,
What might happen in one day's time?

I'm on the coach,
Nearly there,
Do I even dare to stare?
What is it going to be like?

Abigail Holloway (10)
Dingle Primary School

My Best Friend

He's as fast as light
He's as cool as ice.

He's always there for me
He's never sad, he's always happy.

I can just talk to him
Without him making fun of me.

He sticks up for me
If we were in war he would never leave me behind.

And that person is my best friend, Kieran.

Daniel Fellows (11)
Dingle Primary School

My Dogs

My dogs
Are as warm as lava
My dogs
Are as loving as my family
My dogs
Are as loyal as celebs' security guards
My dogs
Are as caring as my parents
My dogs
Are as cool as a surfer
My dogs
Are more precious than a golden ring
My dogs
Are treasure like pirate gold
My dogs
Are the best and would win any test.

Daniel Lamb (11)
Dingle Primary School

Guess Who?

His softness is as if it were cotton wool,
He is as sweet as a lollipop stick,
Bought from the local shop.

I share great joy with this person,
At all times.

His smile brightens up a gloomy day,
Just like the sun,
I love him very much.

He is caring,
Even though he is still young,
He shares all of his kindness with me.

This is my brother; Mattie.

Christopher Round (11)
Dingle Primary School

The Life On The Playground

On the playground life is good
Children play and you can see
Footballs all around flying fast and hard
Like a shooting star
You hear the players shout 'Goal!'
Life on the playground is good
Lush grass and small but cuddly flowers
I love it when summer comes to the playground

All is good on the playground
It is not perfect but to my liking
Some games children play are unfamiliar to me
But I can sense they are happy children who play them
Life on the playground is good
You hear whistles blow and the roaring of happy children

As I sit at the bench curiosity takes me away
I sit for ages until one of my friends comes and taps me
And introduces me with a new game
Life on the playground is good,
Not perfect but to my liking
Laughter and shooting footballs
It is all I ask for

When I am sad I look at children playing
I see their smiles every day
I suddenly feel happy inside
On the playground life is good
Not perfect but to my liking.

Ben Jones (11)
Dingle Primary School

Guess Who?

This person is as soft as a feather,
Yet never shows it.
This person is as cool as a cucumber,
And always will be.
This person is as hard as a brick wall,
Yet you can break his heart just like that.
This person is as annoying as a mosquito,
Yet I still love him.
This person is as loving as my mom,
Yet better.
This person is as popular as the richest human in the world,
Yet doesn't need money.
This person smells like a sewer,
Yet I still love him.
Who is this person?
It's my brother.

Thomas Bowen (11)
Dingle Primary School

Who Is It?

He's loving, he's caring
He's forgiving, he's friendly,
He looks after me!
Who is he?

He's annoying, he's nasty,
He's silly, he's strange,
He lies for me!
Who is he?

He makes me laugh,
He makes me smile,
Who can do all these things,
And be the best?
Who is he?

My brother!

Hayley Siviter (11)
Dingle Primary School

Four Seasons Of The Playground

Spring, spring
New life coming, flowers blooming,
We're on the tarmac playing football
Hoping it's not going to rain
But it doesn't matter we're having too much fun.

Summer, summer
Martin and Ben are playing dens
On the grass
It's that time of year, it's hot
We're getting sunburnt
But it doesn't matter we're having too much fun.

Autumn, autumn
We're in the next school year
Where the leaves are falling
On the ground
We get them up from the floor
And throw them in the air
But it doesn't matter we're having too much fun.

Winter, winter
We are sliding,
Pretending to skate while
Making snowballs
And throwing them at each other
But it doesn't matter we're having too much fun.

Martin Siviter (11)
Dingle Primary School

Who Is She?

She's loving, she's caring, so special to me,
Loyal and friendly,
Lucky me!
Understanding and happy,
Who could it be?
Forgiving and hopeful,
Always there for me.

She's there to cuddle,
When I am down,
She works long hours,
But never makes me frown!

She's kind and helpful, how much does she mean to me?
This much! This much! That's why I write this poem,
This much! This much!
My mum is the best she can be!

Stefanie Ward (10)
Dingle Primary School

Emma!

Emma, Emma is so great
Emma, Emma is my mate

Emma, Emma is the best
Emma, Emma makes no mess

Emma, Emma eats all my sweets
Emma, Emma never cheats

Emma, Emma is my sister
Emma, Emma can be my worst blister

Emma, Emma is so great
I love her more than chocolate cake

Emma, Emma is the best
She is so special to me!

Chloe Gillard (11)
Dingle Primary School

Kittens

K ittens, I have loads!
I just can't keep up,
T abby always claws the furniture,
T oby always tears the curtains,
E very way I love them to bits,
N o one can beat them,
S o I still love them although they're a terror, they're my
little monsters.

Rachel Wood (11)
Dingle Primary School

Venus
(Inspired by 'Night Fishing' by Moira Andrew)

If Venus were an animal it would be a dragon.
Swiftly flying around the sun.
Making the sky bright by its light flame crawling in space.
With its high temperature melting all the stars.
Sneaking through space with its bright torch of light!

Jacob Small   (9)
Eversfield Preparatory School

Mars Is A Dragon
(Inspired by 'Night Fishing' by Moira Andrew)

If Mars were an animal it would be a blue and red dragon.
Flying swiftly around the sun.
It would fly so swiftly it would take a second to orbit the sun.
When Mars glints in the night.
It is the dragon breathing fire.

Robert Woolley (8)
Eversfield Preparatory School

The Crab's Shell

In the sea there was a crab that hadn't got a shell,
He left his home to search for one and bid his friends farewell.
On the way he met a fish that hadn't got a tail,
And saw a pirate ship (it was missing its main sail).
He also saw a surfer; he hadn't got a board,
As well as a speedboat that had nobody aboard.
At last he found a sorceress, who cast a magic spell,
It worked! As almost instantly the crab grew back his shell.
He went back to his home, very vain and proud.
To touch his precious shell, no one was allowed.
He thought that every day he would get masses of fan mail,
Until an accident occurred! He was sat on by a whale!
He woke in casualty but he really felt unwell!
He didn't even realise that he hadn't got his shell.

Tom Lilburn (11)
Eversfield Preparatory School

Fishing

If a fishing rod got a fish,
It would be a fish for sure,
But to choose the bait to catch it is always a challenge,
Cat's whisker, montana or spoon.
If it happens it won't be soon.

Alastair Harryman (9)
Eversfield Preparatory School

If Mars Were A Cat
(Inspired by 'Night Fishing' by Moira Andrew)

If Mars were an animal it would be a cat.
All its multicolour would be her shiny tortoiseshell coat.
She would prowl around the night sky then pounce on all of the stars.
But in all her fun the sun will rise and pussy cat will have to hide.

Jessica Wevill (8)
Eversfield Preparatory School

The Sea Is . . .

The sea is a roaring dragon breathing out fire,
Gobbling humans, swallowing boats
And leaving the scraps at the bottom
Of its two-hundred metre deep stomach.

The sea is a swift moving creature,
Resting only on the beach,
Where it deposits creatures
That it has swallowed.

The sea is a tactical being
Waiting secretly for its prey
And pounces at the last minute
And finishes the victim in one bite.

The sea is as blue as the sky on a sunny day,
As black and angry on a thunderous day,
It sweeps the victims to lie in
Its very deep hollows.

The sea is dangerous and mysterious;
It is unsolvable even by the man that is the brainiest,
The fear and horror by the sea is still unending.

The sea is a treacherous place,
The creatures are just as dangerous,
You never know what it could next be sending.

The sea is deceptive and ingenious,
A force of nature which is unbelievable,
Calm one minute and the next
A raging torrent.

The sea is a bowl of nasty whirlpools
Which sucks you to your death,
From which you will never come back.

Bhavik Parmar (11)
Eversfield Preparatory School

The Moon

(Inspired by 'The Day's Eye' by Pie Corbett)

A gleaming doorknob on a black door
A wrinkly old man's face staring at the sea of clouds
A midnight through the darkness
A white banana on a black plate
A nocturnal animal hiding from Earth
A cold lemon that nobody wants
A block of ungrated cheese out of its pot
An uncoloured tennis ball about to be hit
A grey orange that's just been peeled
A dearest of friend to the stars
A golf ball that's been hit many a time
A broken off chunk of Earth
A rocky rough rigid runway that's red
A two-year-old apple that's been thrown away
A key target to the king of the king of meteors.

Christopher Beaumont-Dark (9)
Eversfield Preparatory School

Lary The Jellyfish

Lary the jellyfish
Was small but quick
Once he stopped eating
And became a stick
When he started to race again
He thought it was too late
It clearly was
Because he was served on a plate.
Now Lary's gone
To some better place
We'll never forget him
Because of his red and yellow sweater.

Sunil Sidhu (10)
Eversfield Preparatory School

Jupiter Is A Chameleon

(Inspired by 'Night Fishing' by Moira Andrew)

If Jupiter were an animal it would be a chameleon.
It has a long tongue of gas that burns the other planets.
It eats all the stars (flies).
It crawls carefully closer to the sun and then hides again.
It clambers from planet to planet, a different colour every time.

John Grimme (8)
Eversfield Preparatory School

Poems Of The Sky

(Inspired by 'Night Fishing' by Moira Andrew)

The moon is a moody old man
Snarling from the night sky.
He opens his wide silver mouth
Shouting out orders to the space all around him.

He tells them to go over there
And he tells the Earth where to go.
The stars just ignore him to annoy him.

Jordan Knight (8)
Eversfield Preparatory School

The Moon

(Inspired by 'Night Fishing' by Moira Andrew)

The moon is a nice old man
Smiling from the night sky
He opens wide his silver mouth
Talking instructions to the stars
Stars listen to the moon speak in the night sky.

Jonathan Oliver (8)
Eversfield Preparatory School

The Sea Is . . .

The sea is a fallen sky
A sinking machine
A huge mirror
A blue zoo
A giant glass of water
A blue panther waiting to pounce on its prey
A nature fire brigade
A blue terminator
A pot of blue paint
A blue treasure chest
A lost world
A blue grave
A blue forest
A blue paradise
A blue cover
An automatic washing machine
A boat's final resting place
A submarine world
A huge bath
A world destroyer
A big swimming pool
A victorious enemy
A blue bin.

Daniel Oliver (10)
Eversfield Preparatory School

Simony The Stingray - Haiku

Simon the stingray,
Is a very nice fellow,
And is respected.

His kind is quite rare,
Since his colour is yellow,
So he's protected.

Ashkaan Golestani (10)
Eversfield Preparatory School

Before The Race

(Inspired by 'Before the Hunt' by Lari Williams)

Nervous times
Help me
Finish line
Guide me to be there first
Stamina
Remember me
May I avoid sloppy techniques and not timing the race
I'm sure I'll win if I run to the best of my ability.

Joseph Jones (9)
Eversfield Preparatory School

If Pluto Were A Puppy

(Inspired by 'Night Fishing' by Moira Andrew)

If Pluto were an animal it would be a red setter puppy.
Pluto's moon would be the dog's grey ball,
Ready to be thrown into the air.
Its coat would shine in the daylight.
He would also guard his home all night
Then have star cereal in the morning.

Bronte Armstrong (8)
Eversfield Preparatory School

Mars

(Inspired by 'Night Fishing' by Moira Andrew)

The planet Mars is red and small like a red ant
It's hot because it creeps fast around the sun
It has got two moons like a red ant has two antennas
It looks at us angrily and it moves away quickly like a red ant
Its nickname is the red rock
And it's like a red evil land.

Ryan Dhadwal (9)
Eversfield Preparatory School

Mars Is A Red Setter

(Inspired by 'Night Fishing' by Moira Andrew)

If Mars were an animal it would be a red setter,
A very cold red setter
Whose fur is always freezing on frosty mornings.
His hair is dusty from rolling in the mud
Wanting someone to tickle his tummy.
But no one does because there is no life around him.
Sometimes he is itchy
Because of the beagle fleas exploring his body.
His days are so long
He has plenty of time to spend howling at his two small moons.

Keelan Fadden-Hopper (9)
Eversfield Preparatory School

The Sun Is A Snake

(Inspired by 'Night Fishing' by Moira Andrew)

If the sun were an animal it would be a snake
The sun is a slithering snake sliding across the sky
The sun slithers and shivers from the moon
The sun lets her star children play at night joking with the moon
She's telling her star children to go to bed at day
She's telling them to shine at night.

Charlotte Wilson (9)
Eversfield Preparatory School

Pluto Is A Penguin

(Inspired by 'Night Fishing' by Moira Andrew)

If Pluto were an animal it would be a tiny penguin
Waddling through the icy cold night sky
Shivering, shyly, skidding on the snow
Pluto's shiny silvery blanket glistening in the starlight
Poor little Pluto, so small and lonely out there on his own.

Sophie Hill (8)
Eversfield Preparatory School

Red Rock

(Inspired by 'Night Fishing' by Moira Andrew)

The planet Mars
Is like a baby dragon
It speeds like a bullet
Round the sun

It is as red as dragon's blazing scales
It doesn't get along with anything
It growls at other planets
It scares the other planets.

Marco Consiglio (9)
Eversfield Preparatory School

Mars Is A Red Squirrel

(Inspired by 'Night Fishing' by Moira Andrew)

If Mars were an animal it would be a red squirrel
Climbing up to Jupiter
Looking for its best friend
Pluto the grey squirrel
Mars goes back into its space
And has moon - nut for tea.

Samantha Deakin (9)
Eversfield Preparatory School

Pluto Penguin

(Inspired by 'Night Fishing' by Moira Andrew)

Pluto is my tiny name
Slowly waddling in space
Into the very dark grey coldness
Like a speck of darkness
Waiting to be noticed.

Harvey Stevens (9)
Eversfield Preparatory School

My First Day At School

(Inspired by 'Before The Hunt' by Lari William)

Best friends
Help me,
Excited children
Invite me,
The headmaster
Greets me,
The family
Encourages me,
On my first day.
As the smell leads
Me to my dinner.
And at the end of the day
Funny friends lead me to my mum.

Meghan Winter (9)
Eversfield Preparatory School

The First Day At School

(Inspired by 'Before The Hunt' by Lari Williams)

The headmaster
Greets me
Excited children
Invite me
Best friends
Help me
The teachers
Look after me
The sweet smell
Goes across school.

Ben Elkin (8)
Eversfield Preparatory School

Moon

(Inspired by 'Before The Hunt' by Moira Andrew)

Moon shouts at the stars telling them where to go
Moon is Earth's son
Bang! Moon has been hit again
Moon is Earth's son
Zoom! Moon is dodging comets going one-hundred miles per hour
Moon is Earth's son.

Ben Thornley (9)
Eversfield Preparatory School

Perimeter Walk

Windy breeze whistling in the air
Swaying as it brushes past

Strolling through the dry leaves
Crunching under your foot

Dazzling daisies, buttery buttercups
Leaf litter lying around

Strolling through the dry leaves
Crunching under your foot

Leaves cracking like a crunchy bar in the warming sun
Flowers swaying in the mild wind

Strolling through the dry leaves
Crunching under your foot

A helicopter buzzes overhead like a busy bee
A bird at the top of a tree singing his socks off!

Sophie Horne
Glynne Primary School

Summertime Has Come

White clouds like icing cover the blue sky.
Clouds like cotton wool cover the blue sky.
Green grass as wet as water shines in the sun.
Grass wet and bright green.
Birds sing beautifully in tune.
Birds chirping, getting louder and louder.
Strolling through the rolling grass.
Strolling through the gleaming grass.
Blades bending in footsteps.
Daisies like sprinkled confetti.
Daisies like confetti lie scattered on the ground.
The trees rustle in the wind.
The trees wave to and fro in the wind.
The day ends with children screaming.

Eve Mallen (9)
Glynne Primary School

The Great Outdoors

All the trees are crowded making sounds like guns at war
But sitting under them is such a bore.

Leaves on the ground, leaves on the trees
Some floating around like busy, busy bees.
Daisies on the ground as white as snow
She tells us to move on but I say, 'No!'
I look around, what can I see?
A little bird buried in the tree making a lovely sound.
Ants on the wood that have been weaved in and out.

All the trees are crowded making sounds like guns at war
But sitting under them is such a bore.

Nathan Jones (9)
Glynne Primary School

Senses All Around Me

What can you smell?
Something like seaweed, showering off the blossom,
What can you smell?
Fresh dribbling grass, young and strong.
Sharp bark chippings, splintering off the tree,
Look all around you, what can you see?
What can you see?
Something like a dragonfly hovering in the sky.
What can you see?
A waving bent branch, a bench made out of a tree.
Sharp bark chippings splintering off the tree,
Look all around you, what can you see?
What can you feel?
Something like tickling, brushing off the hair,
What can you feel?
Burning of the sun, and fluffy flowers stare,
Sharp bark chippings, splintering off the tree,
Look all around you, what can you see?
What can you hear?
Something like flapping, a bird cheeping afar,
What can you hear?
Rain shaker seeds falling, rustling off the leaves,
Sharp bark chippings, splintering off the tree,
Look around you, what can you see?

Bethanie Lowe (9)
Glynne Primary School

Perimeter Walk

Birds singing sweetly in the dappled shade.
Busy bees buzzing around the arena.
Trees rustling in the wind.
The wood moulding in the bright sunshine.
Blades bending in footsteps.
Strolling through the rolling grass.
The scent of flowers fills the air.

Ben Millett-Kirkham (8)
Glynne Primary School

Perimeter Walk

Pointy leaves like porcupine's spikes
Birds twittering sweetly
Scurrying squirrels climbing up trees
Flowers with flattering prettiness.

Leaves chattering
Branches scattering
Blowing through the wind.

The smell of grass is like an exquisite perfume that will last forever
The helicopter above,
Like a buzzing bee, propellers like wings spinning rapidly.

Leaves chattering
Branches scattering
Blowing in the wind.

Eleanor Jordan (9)
Glynne Primary School

It's Wonderful

Strolling through the willow sculpture
Is like a tropical rainforest
With dangling leaves on a tree of dangling branches.
It's beautiful, it's amazing, it's *wonderful!*

Stamping through the field
Is like you're on a big football pitch playing for Brazil
Hearing busy bees and high helicopters
Overlooking houses overhead.
It's beautiful, it's amazing, it's *wonderful.*

Insects scurrying, sky so blue
Smelling the rust on a wheelbarrow.
It's beautiful, it's amazing,
Well then, it's got to be . . . *wonderful!*

Adam Brown (9)
Glynne Primary School

Perimeter Walk

Treading slowly over wavy grass
Stepping across circles of sun, patterns of shade.
A helicopter buzzes overhead like a busy bee in business.
Interwoven willow wood covered with dangling fingers of green.
Daisies, eyes of the day scattered confetti at my feet.
The gentle breeze rustles leaves like an enormous rainmaker.
Hearing the tree whispering in my ear
Leaf litter on the ground, 'Clean me up! Clean me up!'
Candyfloss flying through the sky.

Andrew Meese (9)
Glynne Primary School

Perimeter Walk

Treading slowly over wavy grass
Stepping across circles of sun and patterns of shade.
A helicopter buzzes over like a busy bee on business.
Interwoven willow wood covered with dangling finger of green.
Daisies eyes of the day scattered confetti at my feet.
The gentle breeze rattles leaves like an enormous rainmaker.
Candyfloss clouds scattered in the sea-blue sky.

Russell Homer (9)
Glynne Primary School

Perimeter Walk

Strolling through the willow sculpture,
The leaves fall on me like razors.
The cars are beeping their horns,
The traffic hums in the distance.
The bushes in the field,
Swaying in the wind.
Strolling through the willow sculpture
The leaves fall on me like razors.

Tom Aston (9)
Glynne Primary School

Perimeter Walk

Twittering of birds
Daisies like splodges of paint
A slight whistle in the wind
Trees standing like soldiers
Bendy, twirling branches.

Leaves chattering like an audience in a theatre
Leaves littering the grass.

Smell of the fresh grass
Leaves drooping down like fingers
Black crow is looking with a devious eye
The cars sound like a massive machine.

Leaves chattering like an audience in a theatre
Leaves littering the grass.

Drooping clothes in the back gardens
Scattering children over the field
While the gardener admires his garden
You can just about see a pair of blue shorts in the gaps of the tree.

Isobel Beech (9)
Glynne Primary School

The Perimeter Walk

The wobble of the tree,
All the leaves seem to fall on me,
When I stamp in the grass,
It is like a bent-back blade, broken.
In the distance cars are zooming past,
Helicopters buzzing like bees.
The bushes are rustling
The leaves are racing in the wind.

Joe Sherwood (9)
Glynne Primary School

The Perimeter Walk

Standing under the willow sculpture
It's like a forest full of tiny green bananas!

Strolling in the fresh grass
Blades bending in tiny footsteps.

Close our eyes and we can hear . . .
Tweeting of the birds, buzzing of the helicopter.

Strolling in the fresh grass,
Blades bending in footsteps.

I can smell the new freshly sprouted grass,
And I can smell the dazzling daisies.

Strolling in the fresh grass
Blades bending in tiny footsteps.

The wind is whispering against the trees.

Molly Bowater
Glynne Primary School

Perimeter Walk

Treading slowly over wavy grass
Stepping across circles of sun and patterns of shade.
A helicopter buzzes overhead like a buzzy bee on business
Interwoven willow wood covered with dangling fingers of green.
Daisies, eyes of the day scattered confetti at my feet
The gentle breeze rattles leaves.
Like an enormous rainmaker,
The wind blows into the trees like a rainfall
It feels like I am in an African rainforest.
Candyfloss clouds floating above my head.

Alex Spittle (9)
Glynne Primary School

The Wonder Of Our Five Senses

The humming of a plane high in sky
Like a mechanical bird
Follow the wonderful scent of the food
Ending at the dining hall.

The barking of a dog far, far away
Candy clouds flutter by
The smell of blossom brushing through the air
What a wonderful day!

Hear the tweeting of the birds
Gliding through the air
See sticks on tree branches
Like real moving fingers.

The barking of a dog far, far away
Candy clouds flutter by
The smell of flowers brushing through the air
What a wonderful day!

Scott Badger (9)
Glynne Primary School

The Perimeter Poem

Children chatting
Adults nattering.

Leaves blowing
Branches swaying
Helicopters flying
Birds gliding.

Twigs snapping
Winds rustling.

Leaves blowing
Branches swaying
Helicopters flying
Birds gliding.

Michael Saxon (9)
Glynne Primary School

Perimeter Walk

The green, green grass
The leaves litter the grass
The fragrant smell of flowers
The whistling of the wind.

Birds singing sweetly going to their nests
The silky feel of leaves dangling like fingers
Branches swaying in the breeze.

The bright hot sun
The spikiness of the grass
The feel of gorse grass
The wind blowing people's washing.

Birds singing sweetly going to their nests
The silky feel of leaves dangling like fingers
Branches swaying in the breeze.

That's what you feel, hear, touch and smell on the perimeter walk.

Daniel Evans (8)
Glynne Primary School

About Football

Football is great
It makes you lose some weight
Football is good
It makes you fall in mud
Football is brilliant
Some players are excellent
You can skill them out
The fans all shout
Richardson shoots into the net
I met him on the internet
Football is cool
Fans make you look like a fool
Football is bad
It makes me feel glad.

Ryan Cox (9)
Great Bridge Primary School

The Earth Is Like A Rainbow

The Earth is like a rainbow
With red poppies like red blood.
The Earth is like a rainbow
With red strawberries like red lollipops.

The Earth is like a rainbow
With grapes like green leaves.
The Earth is like a rainbow
With bananas like autumn.

The Earth is like a rainbow
With horses like brown tree trunks.
The Earth is like a rainbow
With the blue seas clean as can be.

The Earth is like a rainbow
With purple literacy books.
The Earth is like a rainbow
With black clouds when it rains.

The Earth is like a rainbow
With the fabulous colours indigo.
The Earth is like a rainbow
With the beautiful colour violet.

The Earth is like a rainbow
With the excellent colour red.
The Earth is like a rainbow
With the good colour black.

Samantha Hubbard (10)
Great Bridge Primary School

Killer Bear

Claws like an eagle,
They roar like a lion
Face of thunder
As hot as an iron.

Snorts like a yak
Eyes like an owl.
Teeth like a cheetah
Has got a ferocious growl.

As strong as an elephant
Fur like a fox.
Can gobble up the fish
Has horns of an ox.

Brain like a dolphin
Can smell like a dog.
Has got hearing like a bat
As heavy as a log.

Aaron Moore (10)
Great Bridge Primary School

Killer Whale

He has teeth like needles,
His bite can kill instantly,
There is no escape, like an octopus is strangling you,
Do not dare to go by him.

It swims like a speedboat,
It attacks faster than an aeroplane,
His tail smacks like a hand,
He is fat, bold and dark grey,
In fights he fights like a sumo-wrestler.

He scares people to death,
People fear him like anything,
Just imagine what he will do to you.

Luke Hosell (9)
Great Bridge Primary School

Football

Football is great
Football is fun
Why not join the football club.

You can play football as a team
You can play football and score goals
Why not do your best if you are in the football team.

Football is cool
Football is class
Why don't you play football in the grass?

You can play football as a team
You can play football and score goals
Why not do your best if you are in a football team?

Football makes you muddy not clean
Football is the best to play when you need to get in a team.

Abigail Golding (11)
Great Bridge Primary School

(Heaven) Good Us Bad (Hell)

Goodness is like when you help an old woman over the road,
Or if you help a friend who's in trouble, that is what good is,
People who have a good heart will make their way to Heaven,
Then you can do what your heart desires.
But badness is something good does not like.
The Devil himself is evil all over
To avoid being evil you should never listen to him and only to God.
Help people cross the road or a dude who fell down.
If you want to be bad and learn nothing,
Grow up with no education, then be my guest
The Devil won't be your friend, he will treat you like dirt,
He'll shoot you down even though you're down.
He'll give you pain, but in Heaven you'll get golden rain.

Brandon Wright (11)
Great Bridge Primary School

Families And Friends

Families will always be there in your life,
They'll keep you safe from harm.
Friends will never leave you,
They'll always make you smile.

Sisters are a part of your family,
They'll sometimes get on your nerves.
You see them in school, at home,
But you'll always know that they'll stand by you.

Brothers are normally very annoying
They'll act like they don't know you.
They'll always boss you around
Brothers ignore you but still look after you.

Friends are always there for you
They are people you can talk to.
You have fun with them at school
Friends help you with your problems.

Families and friends are people you have fun with
They won't leave you on your own.
You can talk to them when you're sad
Families and friends won't let you down.

Sundeep Thandi (11)
Great Bridge Primary School

Goku The Legendary Hero

I wish I was Goku, brave and strong
Battling through battles that have never gone wrong.
With power this world's never seen,
Fighting monsters that are dangerous and mean.
With a really strong son with incredible strength
And he's able to defend himself.
And he fights for good and not for bad
Just for me, his best dad.

Suhail Perager (9)
Great Bridge Primary School

Lions

Lions are huge,
Lions are dangerous,
Lions can also be very scary.

When you go exploring looking for lions
You should bring a car
So they don't catch you.

Don't be scared,
Don't be afraid,
Do whatever your captain says.

If you are filming lions
Always stay in a faraway position.

Don't bring children,
Don't bring kids,
Don't bring anyone that is under fifteen.

The danger of bringing children
They may wander off and you will not find them.

Always watch your back,
Always be careful
Always run when you are chased.

When you are being chased by a lion
You quickly jump in your car.

Ajay Singh (11)
Great Bridge Primary School

My Friend

My friend Luke ripped his pants on the way to school
He nipped down the corner shop and bought some PVA glue
When he got it he went home and went to bed with his favourite ted.
The next morning he woke up,
He had bacon and a whole glass of 7Up,
He told us he had fixed his pants
When I went to his house he had all sorts of plants.

Awais Younis (10)
Great Bridge Primary School

Dogs And Cats

Dogs are loveable to you
As cuddly as a teddy
They are very friendly
As cute as a cat.

You can take dogs anywhere
But keep them away from cats
They will get jealous and upset
If you don't give them attention.

Cats are very sweet
But if you have fish your cat will eat them.
They are very sly.

Cats hate budgies, so beware of the dangers
Or the next time you see your budgie
He might be dead!

Dogs and cats don't mix together,
So keep them away from each other
Or there might be chaos
Do not buy a dog or cat together!

Samantha Oakley (11)
Great Bridge Primary School

Clouds In A Summer's Breeze

The clouds float peacefully
In the summer's air.
Watch them float,
Like a boat in a calm sea.
Watch the sun float by them,
So that they shine and glow.
When it turns to winter the clouds grow grey,
So go in and watch them another day.

Stacey Nock (10)
Great Bridge Primary School

A School Playground

A loud and noisy playground
With children all around
Everyone is running
Acting like a clown.

The sun is shining
The sky is bright
All of the little children, what a pretty sight.
All of the boys are cheering and shouting at the football
All of the girls are dancing, skipping and having fun.

Then the playground becomes empty,
All of the children are learning
Before it all happens again.

Sarah Hampson (10)
Great Bridge Primary School

Swans

Swans are beautiful like water trickling gently,
They swim freely around and follow each other.
They're as white as snowflakes,
They also belong to the fairy queen.

Sometimes they can be harmful,
And hurt you very much.
So if you're out walking by the riverside,
Be careful or you might die!

Swans might look deceiving,
But you should really know what they're like.
They might be as sweet as an angel,
Or as nasty as they like!

Chloe Hadley (10)
Great Bridge Primary School

If I Could Be . . .

If I could be a worm
I would squiggle down in the dirt with my slimy body.

If I could be a dolphin
I would swim all over the sea
And meet new sea creatures and even have tea.

If I could be a book
I would express myself loud and clear.

If I could be a clown
I would make people laugh in my funny costume.

But because I can't be any of them
I will have to stay as the plain old monkey I have always been
Well . . . *that's fine with me!*

Charlotte Cox (10)
Great Bridge Primary School

School

At school it is really, really cool
You can talk to your mates
Or accidentally be a fool
You can hang around by the gates
Until the school bell rings
And the children run around
The teacher has dropped all her things
You can't hear anything, there's not a sound
As the day goes on everything is still
Except from inside where the children are working
It's home time they are walking down the hill
Some children are around there lurking.

Rebecca Hughes (10)
Great Bridge Primary School

Dream

I dreamt that I was soaring,
Soaring over the world,
I dreamt that I was soaring,
When the night was cold.

I didn't feel secure and sure,
As I drifted up high,
To see a shimmering figure
Floating in the sky.

Then she turned and disappeared
In the darkness below,
Then it happened as I feared,
The scene changed from top to toe.

I dreamt that I was falling,
Falling in a hole,
I dreamt that I was falling,
I felt a burning in my soul.

Then the darkness hit me,
It hit me in the eye,
Then unfortunately I couldn't see,
But I heard a faint cry.

Then an icy hand reached out,
And touched my finger's tip.
Soon she hushed me and didn't shout,
And placed her fingers on her lips.

I dreamt my mother was holding me,
So no harm came to me.
I dreamt my mother was holding me
From Heaven . . . to protect me.

Thonima Mahbub (11)
Great Bridge Primary School

Fire Bell

Fire bell ringing, walk outside,
Fire brigade comes,
Get their hoses,
Squirt water,
Put out the fire,
Check the school is fine,
Give out the registers,
Make sure everyone is here,
It goes off two more times,
We all go out two more times
And they give out the registers,
We go back in to finish our work,
And I hope it never happens again.

Some people thought it was funny,
But I thought it was dangerous,
Just in case someone wasn't there,
The teachers checked,
Everyone was there,
It was just a fault,
That set off the alarm,
And then it didn't go off again.

Natalie Oakes (10)
Great Bridge Primary School

Seasons Out My Window

Winter flakes
Make me shake
Long spring showers
Bring my flowers
Summer breeze
Makes me sneeze
Autumn's weather
Makes me dither.

Heidi McManus (11)
Lindens Primary School

Lies, Lies, Lies

Why do you have to lie?
Why, why, why?
I mean there is no point to,
Lie, lie and lie.

All I ever hear of you is not the truth
But a lie,
You lied the other day at the shop,
You even lied about the pop,

I bet you cannot tell the truth for one day
And when you give up it's time to pay
I will remember that day
Forever while I may
Lie, why, cry, for all I care
'There's a big, fluffy bear'
Liar!

Toni Stevens (11)
Lindens Primary School

The Castle Fort

The castle fort
The castle fort
A piece of history
Powerful, strong, glorious
Like a dark figure
Constantly seen by stars
I feel proud and brave
The castle fort
With memories of dying,
Hating, glory and loss.

Samuel Crawford (11)
Lindens Primary School

Baldilocks And The Three Hairs

There once was a girl called Baldilocks,
Who only had three hairs.
They always used to tease her,
And made her take dares.

One day she decided to cut her hair off,
And when she got to the barber shop,
She caught a terrible cough.

The cough got really bad,
That she couldn't even talk.
And then she caught a cold,
And she couldn't even walk.

The next week she was better,
And went back to the shop.
When they cut off all her hair,
She dropped dead in a shock.

Kiran Gill (11)
Lindens Primary School

The Hot Air Balloon

Hovering in the clear blue sky.
Way up in the clouds
And the birds fly by.

The hot air balloon
Floats past everything you see
I think that's really exciting to me.

The hot air balloon
Have a ride
It's very high though
Are you sure you want a go?

Amber Robinson (10)
Lindens Primary School

School Days

I hate school
Silly, foolish game
Why do I have to go to school?
I can't face the shame.

Computer days are fun
Same with maths and art
All I do is sit in the classroom
Why don't I just take part?

I hate English
Silly, foolish game
Why do I have to go to school?
I can't face the shame.

I really want to know you
Very well indeed
So read it, enjoy it
To get information you need.

Shanice Prince (11)
Lindens Primary School

Sneaky Animals!

Dogs are cute and sweet.
They always bite your *disgusting* feet!
Pigs are very smelly
And have a *big, fat belly!*
Cats are sneaky and sly.
They bite your dangling ties.
Birds like to fly . . .

              h
        g
     i
Up h   in the sky.

Katie Perkins (11)
Lindens Primary School

Fireworks

F iring rockets
I ncredible sights
R eally hot bonfires
E xtraordinary sparklers
W onderfully exciting
O range and red
R eady to impress
K aboom! Kaboom! Zoom!
S oaring high.

Sophie Fisher (10)
Lindens Primary School

What Am I?

I am loud
I float like a cloud
I am cool but not very small
My habitat is hot
I look like a dot
What am I?

Josh Finegan (11)
Lindens Primary School

My Pet

My rabbit has short fur
But he doesn't growl, bark or purr
All he does is sit in his hutch
Eating carrots and other stuff
Billy Joe is his name
He is very friendly and extremely tame.

Jade Morris (10)
Lindens Primary School

Dogs

Dogs come in all shapes and sizes
They are meant to be a man's best friend
But when they mess in other people's garden
The friendship could go round a completely different bend!

But dogs aren't just for Christmas
They are for your whole life complete
So even when they do go a bit crazy
Don't throw them out on the street.

Dogs come in all different breeds
From the tiny chihuahua to the huge Great Dane
And just because the bulldog's most ugly
Doesn't mean he deserves the most pain.

All dogs deserve TLC
They all need the best they get
From a nice bit of breakfast in the morning,
To a warm bed at night
And a nice big hug
When dribbled on from another dog's bite.

Laura Murphy (11)
Lindens Primary School

Moms

Moms are like red roses getting brighter every day
They are honest and truthful to you
They protect you and hold you in their arms
When you have arguments they always say they love you
But one thing they don't do is lie
They always cook you dinner
They sometimes cry
They go places with you no matter what
Moms are lovely.

Catherine Ball (11)
Lindens Primary School

SATs

We work and sweat all year round,
To sit in a room without a sound.
We should be out in the sunshine,
Not sitting watching the time.

We learnt our tables upside down,
But the questions just make us frown.
The English questions were also bad,
So when it finished we were glad.

What are these SATs really about?
I asked my dad, he had his doubts.
What happened to football, cricket and fun?
Please let me get out into the sun.

Richard Wheeler (11)
Lindens Primary School

Fruit

Fruit is very nice,
You have it, one, two, three times a day,
The problem is when you pay,
When you buy them you have to keep them high 'cause of mice.

You could say you couldn't live without fruit,
'Cause of the nutrition of course,
You don't have to eat them with force either,
That's what's good about fruit.

Oranges, apples, bananas,
There's a whole wide range of them,
About a hundred or more,
Fruit, fruit, fruit.

Ben Whatley (11)
Lindens Primary School

How Come?

How come adults must work all day?
How come they must live in flats?
How come they have so little to say?
How come they must pay lots of tax?

How come children must go to school?
How come they spend hours on looks?
How come they care about looking cool?
How come they are forced to read books?

How come people are the way they are?

Jozef Doyle (11)
Lindens Primary School

Anger

Anger is red like Mars
It sounds like screeching gulls
It tastes like fire scorching the walls of your mouth
It smells like the worst rotten egg
It looks like a huge volcano, sitting on the brink of eruption
It feels like a sharp searing knife, cutting deep into your skin
It reminds me of my teacher!

Megan Saul (11)
Lindens Primary School

Tan The Circus Man

Tan the circus man, tired, in stress,
His elephant ran away and he was in a real mess,
For him life was a misery,
The weather was blustery,
The circus show was on the twenty-eighth of May
And that was the day after today.

Shiv Parekh (11)
Lindens Primary School

Tor Chang The Dragon

T he dragon is green
O range fire he breathes
R uining anything in his path

C hanging forests into ash
H overing above cities
A lighting poor kitties
N efarious is he
G igantic and free!

Oliver Willis (10)
Lindens Primary School

A Seasons Poem

Spring: flowers trying to burst.
Spring: birds come to sing.
Spring: planting my vegetables.
Spring: flowers do a ring.

Summer: children swimming in the pool.
Summer: children playing outside.
Summer: children come in to cool.
Summer: children playing inside.

Autumn: leaves change colour.
Autumn: wind blows.
Autumn: wind chases leaves.
Autumn: everyone's door is closed.

Winter: snow is falling.
Winter: dropping snow.
Winter: play in snow.
Winter: play a game called snow pow.

Sukhpreet Nainu (9)
Little Heath Primary School

My Time Poem

Spring: flowers starting to peep.
Spring: baby birds calling their mothers.
Spring: looking at the lovely sight.

Summer: the sun is blazing.
Summer: children playing.
Summer: lying in the sun.

Autumn: bare trees.
Autumn: leaves shuffling
Autumn: walking through the wind.

Elisha Jawaid (9)
Little Heath Primary School

My Time Poem

Bedtime: my favourite programme.
Bedtime: cars passing.
Bedtime: sink my drowsy head.

Midnight: dreams fill my imagination.
Midnight: hear the noises of my fantasies.
Midnight: roll from side to side.

Morning: the brightly coloured walls surround me.
Morning: I hear the voice of my soul.
Morning: I take a break to relax.

Karenjit Kaur Somal (8)
Little Heath Primary School

Where Are All The Kids?

I'm waiting for the bell to ring,
For other children, to laugh and sing,
For them to dash outside and play,
But wait . . . no one's here today!

No wait, I must be wrong,
I heard the choir chanting songs,
They stared at me all through maths,
Desperate to get out of class.

What? Ice! Skipping across my face?
White powder all over the place!
No children laughing, or singing songs
When the bell has already gone!

What happened? I'm so confused,
Are they already being amused?
I mean, half of me is a frozen lake!
I'm a playground for goodness sake!

An hour and a half of the day is mine!
This powder can't be a good sign,
I'm bored to death! I'm frozen too,
And there's nothing else to do!

Maybe I'll chat to the swing set,
Or talk it up with the slide
Well I've got nothing else to do
Until the others come outside.

Nina Kapur (10)
Little Sutton Primary School

Feelings

Anger is a volcano ready to explode,
It makes me scream my thoughts out loud
Even though I remain silent
Getting madder every time the clock ticks.
Anger makes tiny knives behind my eyes
And tries to force out tears
It always succeeds.

Hope fights my anger away
It is the light shining on my hopelessness
It always comes out first until
World War III erupts again.

Sadness fills my mind
Mixing my already mangled thoughts
I cannot control it
Sometimes it bursts free
My actions are uncontrollable, anger returns
I am angry with myself
And so the cycle goes on
And on . . .
Evermore.

Samantha Hobbs (11)
Little Sutton Primary School

Depression

Depression, depression,
Is a bad expression.
It takes control of your mind,
It will never ever be kind.

If depression enters your head,
Your facial expression will drop down dead.
When it enters your happy face,
Do not show it and lock it in a case!

Madison Millward-Murray (11)
Little Sutton Primary School

School Play

Oh no, we are doing a school play,
It is where the parents have to pay,
I think it is really boring,
Sometimes I can hear the teachers' snoring!

Rehearsals are such a bore,
It really makes me want to snore,
I am a pig in the play,
I don't see why I should stay.

Singing, oh please!
It makes you want to scream,
Oh those teachers are mean,
When we are bad they turn green!

I don't see why I should do the play,
We didn't ask to do it anyway,
Imagine Miss Austin dressed very queer,
Dressed only in cling film- cheer!

Alexandra Paxton (11)
Little Sutton Primary School

Things In School

When I first went to school,
I saw Mrs Morton wait at the door.
We went in and waited a while
Until Mrs Morton started to smile.
Teacher.

At the break time I didn't know what was going on,
Until Iona came and we played football all day long.
Friend.

Those were most of the things I did in school today
To be honest, they were OK!

Borbala Balint (11)
Little Sutton Primary School

Teachers Vs Pupils

Children in the classroom,
Children in the hall,
Got to get away from here,
They're driving me up the wall.

Ah! In the staffroom,
Now that's the place to be,
Drinking tea and coffee,
Hope they save some for me.

Climbing a tree,
How exhilarating it is for me,
Teachers call me down,
With more than a frown.

They give me detention,
For a couple of weeks,
They think I'm bad,
I think they're mad.

Teachers, teachers,
Think they are great,
Just because they can keep us in after school,
When we come in late.

Children, children,
How they are mean,
Keeping me in after school,
So I miss Mr Bean!

Here comes the headteacher,
What's she going to say?
Children, teachers,
Go away!

Arjun Singh Mann (11)
Little Sutton Primary School

Who Am I?

I'm a big fierce animal,
Like the sea,
Raging and roaring fierce,
That's me!

I'm black and orange,
With claws so big to fight,
That when I come to catch my prey,
I'll pounce with all my might.

I have very sharp teeth with which,
To munch my lovely prey,
And then I find a comfy cavern,
Where I curl up and lay.

I'm part of the cat family,
I can be incredibly quiet,
But if I want I can be loud,
Who am I?

Fiona Rollings (11)
Little Sutton Primary School

Playground

On the old large playground
Excited children play,
Laughing, games and having fun,
In the sky is a huge bright sun
Fun for everyone.

On the grassy big field,
Lives a big fat ball,
Being a boring old fool,
Waiting for fun.

Down in the corner of the field,
Is a large wooden frame,
With the children having a game
Fun for everyone.

Jemma Westgate (11)
Little Sutton Primary School

Life And Death

What do you think of death?
Your dying moments, your last breath.
What do you think of life?
Just a dimension full of struggles and strife.

Which do you think is worse?
Do you praise life and think death is cursed?
Do you think death pulls you in
To burning places full of sin?

So what does life do?
What is in it for you?
Something perfect, something good,
Or is it just the Grim Reaper with a white hood?

Which would you choose?
Do you want to win or lose
In the game of life?
Or should we say,
The game of life and death?

Chloe O'Carroll (11)
Little Sutton Primary School

Teachers

Some teachers can be evil,
But others can be nice,
That is the way they are,
When they deal with a mathematical dice.

Some teachers are dumb,
But others are smart,
But believe it or not,
They can teach us art.

As the whistle goes, they jump from their desks,
That is the time they must get dressed,
As the children come up the stairs,
They all do their hair.

Eleanor Biggs (10)
Little Sutton Primary School

Hate

He lurks in the black depths of your mind.
With each passing second, he grows stronger.
When Happiness recedes, Hate readies himself.
For soon, his time for action will come.
Suddenly, he pounces - and fights Love till it retreats.
All hope has nearly faded now, as Hate will stop at nothing.
Love may be down, but not yet out.
And a glimmer of hope emerges from despair.
So in a final battle, the two forces clash.
Each side fights on, unwilling to cease.
But suddenly, the fight has finished.
Love was victorious - all evil has gone!
And yet . . .
Hate remains, immoral as ever.
And, in the black depths of your mind
He waits . . .

Richard Robinson (11)
Little Sutton Primary School

Light Poem

It showers the world with love and joy
It destroys the hatred in every girl and every boy
Darkness can't evade it, not for long
It forgives every sin, no matter what we've done wrong
It stops our desires, turning into lust
It allows us to learn, it allows us to trust.

No matter what we say
No matter what we do
There's always light coursing through you
From the flick of a switch
To the morning sun
It finds its way into everyone.

Andrew Tsiappourdhi (10)
Little Sutton Primary School

Four Seasons

Spring is . . .
A cuddle,
New beginning muddle,
Daffodils blooming,
Summer looming,
Sweets in your mouth,
Holidays down south.

Summer is . . .
Strawberries and ice cream,
The tropical sea's gleam,
Getting a tan,
Using a fan,
A shining sun,
A truck load of fun.

Autumn is . . .
The crunch of leaves,
The jumper gran weaves,
Apple pie,
Summer's gone - sigh,
A new school,
Playing the fool.

Winter is . . .
An old year's end,
Santa's letter to send,
Christmas cheer,
A robin you hear,
Snow days,
Misty haze.

Each season great, for each a long wait.

Joanna Errington (11)
Little Sutton Primary School

My Teacher Is A Clown

My teacher is a clown,
To make everybody stare.
She has a big red nose,
And wavy bright green hair.

My teacher is a clown,
And almost nobody knows.
That underneath her shoes,
Are smelly purple toes.

My teacher is a clown,
She has the palest skin.
Once a shy boy came to school,
And kicked her on the shin.

My teacher is a clown,
She has microscopic ears.
And if she sees a boring child,
She bursts into tears.

My teacher is a clown,
She has funny dark blue eyes.
But when she gets angry,
She splats everyone with pies.

My teacher is a clown,
She has giant floppy shoes.
School is finished now,
So now she's on the loose!

Ben Griffiths (10)
Little Sutton Primary School

Ballet Shoes

I fit on someone's feet,
I can always feel the beat
As someone does me up
It tickles my pink lace,
And the beautiful smile sitting in its place.
What am I?

Her super-soft fingers as she puts me on,
As she dances swiftly to the beautiful song.
The magnificent steps, as she rhymes and mimes in depth.
What am I?

The long thin feet that slip inside,
As if they're waiting to suddenly hide.

The tall thin dance teacher telling me what to do,
Coughing and spluttering like she's got the flu!
What am I?

Brogan Hadland (11)
Little Sutton Primary School

The Dance Studio

I glided into the room in search of my place,
Looked down at my feet which were rearing away.
The music came on, my chin lifted up and I was ready to go . . .
It seemed like my body and feet had run away
And were dancing to the beat, in my mind I couldn't follow.
The beat of music howled in my ears and ran around in my head.
Faces looked down at me, staring at my newly polished shoes.
The room was filled with happiness also with life.
The mirrors were pounding and ballet bars sprinting,
Oh how I feel alive.
This joy to be dancing is a bird spreading its wings
Waiting to spread its feathers and lift off, while chirping and singing.
Oh how I love to be here in this dance studio!

Bethany Davis-Jones (11)
Little Sutton Primary School

Water

Big, blue and wonderful
It's everywhere around
You can never find it on the land
Or never on the ground

It can fall from the clouds
Up high in the sky
And if it wasn't in this world
Everything would be dry

We're very lucky to have this thing
With us here today
'Cause it keeps our bones all big and strong
So that we can play

So if you ever use too much
And found that you've ran out
Then maybe think twice before you take
This precious thing from its spout!

Water . . . you can never have too much!

Ellie Iezekiel (10)
Little Sutton Primary School

Darkness

Darkness: it prowls the world and shadows it with fear,
It has razor-sharp teeth with maroon-red blood dripping,
Slowly, from its mouth.
The whole world living in fear,
When will it stop?

Suddenly, in the east, a little flicker of hope arises.
The flowers start to open,
The birds begin to sing
And the darkness rules no more.
It hides somewhere that nobody knows,
Waiting, just waiting ready to emerge once again . . .

Abbie Dosell (11)
Little Sutton Primary School

Life Doesn't Frighten Me At All

Lifts that won't stop,
Santa that might pop,
Life doesn't frighten me at all.
All alone in the dark,
Dreaming of a man-eating shark,
Life doesn't frighten me at all.

The dog next door,
Santa on my bedroom floor,
Life doesn't frighten me at all.
In a shop all alone,
Strangers on the kitchen phone,
Life doesn't frighten me at all.

I go *rah!*
They run far
I won't sob
That's my job
They have a row
Oh, they smell
Life doesn't frighten me at all.

Being stuck in a massive tree,
Ghost that might jump out at me,
Life doesn't frighten me at all.
Wasps on my head,
Little rats in my bed,
Life doesn't frighten me at all.

Life doesn't frighten me at all,
Not at all,
Not at all
Life doesn't frighten me at all.

Emma Hall (10)
Little Sutton Primary School

Life Doesn't Frighten Me At All

Spiders on the wall,
Santa in the mall
Life doesn't frighten me at all.
Bees and wasps stinging me,
Frankenstein on the TV.
Life doesn't frighten me at all.

Monsters waiting in anticipation
Trains zooming past in the station.
Life doesn't frighten me at all.
Hoovers making a horrific sound,
Thunder clapping all around.
Life doesn't frighten me at all.

I start to play,
Hope they go away
I stand tall
They shrink small
I say *'No!'*
So they go
Life doesn't frighten me at all.

Screeching gates
A gang of mates
Life doesn't frighten me at all
Mummy and Daddy in a fight
Me in my bed alone at night
Life doesn't frighten me at all.

Life doesn't scare me,
Never ever
Never ever
Life doesn't frighten me at all.

Abigail Holt (10)
Little Sutton Primary School

Life Doesn't Frighten Me At All

Mrs Pipken is like a big bad wolf,
And all she likes is boring golf.
She doesn't frighten me at all.
She has teeth like a witch,
And makes you wear jumpers that really itch.
She doesn't frighten me at all.

She makes you stay in if you talk in class,
And gives you detention if you play on the brass.
She doesn't frighten me at all.
She wears horrible jumpers that make you laugh,
And if she smiles it would make you bargh!
She doesn't frighten me at all.

I go *hee, hee*!
She keeps a close eye on me.
I just wink,
She doesn't blink.
I start to stare,
She gets scared.
She doesn't frighten me at all.

If you are naughty or play around,
She'll send you straight out of the school ground.
She doesn't frighten me at all.
If you saw her you'd think it was a nightmare,
And you should see the state of her hair!
She doesn't frighten me at all.

She doesn't frighten me at all.
Not at all,
Not at all,
And she never will.

Keeley Smith (10)
Little Sutton Primary School

The Seven (Not So) Deadly Sins

Sloth is a runner,
Faster than fast,
He is the first, sadly not the last,
Of the seven deadly sins.

Wrath's always happy,
He'd never shout,
If you were to meet him, you'd never doubt,
He's a seven deadly sin.

Gluttony's stick thin,
He hates to eat,
He'd never enjoy a tasty treat,
He's a seven deadly sin.

Envy's so selfless,
Jealous, not him,
His outlook on life is never grim,
He's a seven deadly sin.

Lust doesn't want,
He'll go without,
He is so proud that he'll scream and shout,
I'm a seven deadly sin!

Greed never wants more,
To charity he gives,
On the edge of life is where he lives,
He's a seven deadly sin.

Pride is the seventh,
Humble to most,
Unlike his comrades he hates to boast.
The sins.

Alice Veitch (11)
Little Sutton Primary School

Lost In The Tropics

Lost in the tropics,
That's where I was.
Alone in the world,
Separate from you,
In the deadly air.

Lost in the tropics,
That's where I was.
Monkeys howling, bees buzzing,
Nowhere to run,
Nowhere to hide.

Lost in the topics,
That's where I was.
The rumbling river,
Calling, calling,
Calling me to it.

Lost in the river,
That's where I was.
Sinking, sinking
Down to the bottom,
Down to my final resting place.

Suzanne Everett (11)
Little Sutton Primary School

Rainforest

R ainforest roots grow and die,
A nchor chains clutch to the trees,
 I n and out when they cry,
N ew trees grow with the breeze,
F orest trees sigh,
O rang-utans freeze,
R ed eyes try to pry,
E eerier silences start to sneeze,
S miling birds learn to be sly,
T oucans, crocodiles, snakes too, all live in their natural habitat.

Harmeet Chatha (11)
Little Sutton Primary School

Life Doesn't Frighten Me

A life worthy height,
Is not always right,
Life doesn't frighten me at all.
A bath with a plug,
Spider in a mug,
Life doesn't frighten me at all.

Thunderstorms appear,
Lightning can be here.
They don't frighten me at all.
The oozing of blood,
Squelching maroon mud,
That doesn't frighten me at all.

I go bang,
Monsters with a fang,
All run away,
After coming in May,
I won't scream
They're all mean,
Life doesn't frighten me at all.

Clowns with a painted face,
Just stand there in disgrace,
Life doesn't frighten me at all,
Because if I scream at all,
You won't hear anymore,
Life doesn't frighten me at all.

Life doesn't frighten me at all,
Not at all,
Not at all,
Life will never frighten me at all.

Deborah Pryor (10)
Little Sutton Primary School

Life Doesn't Frighten Me At All

Hairy spiders all around,
Dead people underground,
Life doesn't frighten me at all.
Sharp scissors chopping my hair,
Dirty car fumes in the air,
Life doesn't frighten me at all.

Lost in the night,
Ghosts that give you a fright,
They don't frighten me at all.
Bright staring eyes,
Nasty men in disguise,
They don't frighten me at all.

I go rah,
They run far,
I make fun,
And watch them run,
I won't weep,
They'll fall asleep,
I just smile,
They go wild,
Life doesn't frighten me at all.

The roaring vacuum under the stairs,
Grandad's grey and greasy hairs,
Life doesn't frighten me at all.
Big swooping birds,
Charging herds,
Life doesn't frighten me at all.

Amelia Tipper (10)
Little Sutton Primary School

Bullies

Bullies, bullies always there,
Bullies, bullies here to scare.
Bullies, bullies just don't care,
Bullies, bullies always dare!

The bullies are here and,
They're out of control,
The bullies are here and,
I've just gone cold.

What can I do? I'm going to fall,
What can I do? I feel so small,
There are just like flares burning,
All night and burning all day,
Until the day breaks!

I am so happy that I'm on my own
The bullies have gone and left me alone.
But do not forget there is a moral to this poem
Tell your parents and all will be fine
Don't forget the world is divine!

Alex Nash (10)
Little Sutton Primary School

The Guns Come Out

I'm loud but dangerous,
I can be silent but deadly,
I can be seen in rare shops,
The enemy can be down before he arrives
When I'm aggressive all I see is blood
Your heart will stop as soon as I penetrate your soul.
What am I?

Aaron Bagga (11)
Little Sutton Primary School

Life Doesn't Frighten Me At All

The howling wind knocking against my window,
Whistling through cracks in the front door,
Life doesn't frighten me at all.
The curtain waving as if someone is there,
It's hitting me like someone trying to grab me,
Life doesn't frighten me at all.

Shadows of wolves on my bedroom wall,
Very strange noises coming from down the hall,
That doesn't frighten me at all.
Creeping things in the dark,
Dreaming of man-eating sharks,
No they don't frighten me at all.

I scream very loud,
At ghosts in a cloud,
I just play,
While they find a way,
To get me into their lair,
But I just forget they're there,
Life doesn't frighten me at all.

Spiders and snakes getting very close to me,
Running very fast and slithering through grass,
That doesn't frighten me at all.
The thought of someone watching you,
Jumping out from behind your bedroom door,
That doesn't frighten me at all.

Life doesn't frighten me at all,
Not at all,
Not at all,
Life doesn't frighten me at all.

Rebecca Jarvis (10)
Little Sutton Primary School

Life Doesn't Frighten Me

An extremely scary, steep height,
Huge ghosts, what a sight,
Life doesn't frighten me at all.
A sternly shouting, frightening teacher,
And my mum when I can't reach her,
Life doesn't frighten me at all.

The bath water swirling round,
The bellowing lawnmower sound,
They don't frighten me at all.
The cliff-drop spiralling stairs going down,
The revolting strange face of a clown,
No, they don't frighten me at all.

I make a face
So they race
I won't run
They're off like a gun
I pretend they aren't there
They lose all their hair
Life really doesn't frighten me at all.

Vampire spiders in my home,
Wondering and wandering all alone,
Life doesn't frighten me at all.
The howling wind roaring by,
Clouds making scary shapes in the sky,
No, they don't frighten me at all.

Life doesn't frighten me at all,
Not at all,
Not at all,
Life doesn't frighten me at all.

Daniel Karandikar (10)
Little Sutton Primary School

Life Doesn't Frighten Me!

Fireworks erupting at night,
Bloodthirsty spiders giving me a fright,
Life doesn't frighten me at all.
Eyes glaring at me,
The vast crashing of the sea,
Life doesn't frighten me at all.

Strangers in the park,
All alone in the dark,
Life doesn't frighten me at all.
Surrounded by enormous crowds,
The thought of falling clouds,
Life doesn't frighten me at all.

I stand tall,
Strong as a wall,
Afraid of school,
People think they're cool,
Big kids in a crowd,
Making their voices loud,
Life doesn't frighten me at all.

Drowning in a canal,
The thoughts of Hell,
Life doesn't frighten me at all.
Being swarmed by bats,
Bitten by contagious rats,
Life doesn't frighten me at all.

Life doesn't frighten me at all,
Not at all,
Not at all,
Life doesn't frighten me at all.

Harvey George (10)
Little Sutton Primary School

Life Doesn't Frighten Me At All!

Would I ever heal
If I were a monster meal?
Life doesn't frighten me at all.
Floorboards creaking
Monsters sneaking
Life doesn't frighten me at all.

Horrible pictures on the wall
Creepy crawlies down the hall
No, they don't frighten me at all.
Razor-sharp teeth on a dog
Horrible guts out of a frog
They don't frighten me at all.

I shout *boo!*
To make them shoo.
I nick their money
But they don't think it's funny
I won't scream
I just dream
Life doesn't frighten me at all.

All alone in the park
A lot of strangers in the dark
Life doesn't frighten me at all.
Horrible wolves waiting to see
If they're having me for their tea
Life doesn't frighten me at all.

Not at all
Not at all
Life doesn't frighten me at all.

Marcos Padilla (10)
Little Sutton Primary School

Life Doesn't Frighten Me

Scared of the dark
Spiders in the park
Life doesn't frighten me at all.
Monsters under my bed
Creepy crawlies in my head
Life doesn't frighten me at all.

Going fast in the car
Ghosts far and far
They don't frighten me at all.
Really big bees
Stinging me on my knees
That doesn't frighten me at all.

I go *moo*
Make them run too
I pull silly faces
Make them have races
I won't laugh
Make them go daft
Life doesn't frighten me at all.

A big whirlpool
Falling in the hall
Life doesn't frighten me at all.
Being on my own
Doesn't frighten me at all
Life doesn't frighten me at all.

Life doesn't frighten me at all,
Not at all,
Not at all,
Life doesn't frighten me at all.

Anisha Bagga (10)
Little Sutton Primary School

Life Doesn't Frighten Me

Vacuums down the hall,
Children with a ball,
Life doesn't frighten me at all.
A big plug hole,
A big black mole,
Life doesn't frighten me at all.

The toilet flushing,
Mommy's blushing,
Life doesn't frighten me at all.
A big open fire,
My friend Mia,
Life doesn't frighten me at all.

I go *roar*
They run far,
I pull faces,
They have races,
I won't sob,
They get a job,
Life doesn't frighten me at all.

A whirling pool,
A great huge mule,
Life doesn't frighten me at all.
The squelching mud,
An enormous slug,
Life doesn't frighten me at all.

Life doesn't frighten me at all,
Not at all,
Not at all,
Life doesn't frighten me at all.

Sarah Kelly (10)
Little Sutton Primary School

Scared?

Deceiving people pondering by,
Thieves in court who just deny,
Telling tales I do not do.
Getting lost in Sainsbury's,
Boys who get you and always tease,
Telling tales I do not do.

Knickers with creepy-crawlies in,
Black cats in the rubbish bin,
Telling tales I do not do.
The washing machine getting your socks,
A lion nipping your mother's frocks,
Telling tales I do not do.

I go, *go!*
They feel low
Time passes by
They turn shy
Nothing left to do
Now they have flu
Telling tales I do not do.

White winter ghosts on the run,
Creepy clowns saying, 'Fun, fun, fun!'
Telling tales I do not do.
Vile poison in my reach,
Witches cackle and witches screech,
Telling tales I do not do.

No I don't,
No I don't,
Telling tales I do not do.

Hayley Chapman (10)
Little Sutton Primary School

Life Doesn't Frighten Me At All

Fireworks exploding at night
Bloodthirsty wrestlers give me a fright
Life doesn't frighten me at all.
The word death and die
Eyes staring at me
Life doesn't frighten me at all.

Mean old Cinderella
Being cut up by a propeller
They don't frighten me at all.
Dragons breathing fire
Being called a liar
Life doesn't frighten me at all.

I go *raa*
They run far
I just laugh
At the cow's calf
I won't cry
To get a pie
Life doesn't frighten me at all.

The horrible teachers at school
The thought of not being cool
Life doesn't frighten me at all.
Monsters in the park
Ghosts in the dark
Life doesn't frighten me at all.

Life doesn't frighten me at all
Not at all
Not at all
Life doesn't frighten me at all.

Andrew Smith (10)
Little Sutton Primary School

The Playground

As the day goes by
My life passes by
On the dark and
Misty playground.

I make friends
I lose friends
On the dark and
Misty playground.

As I leave my desk
I see my friends play
On the dark and
Misty playground.

I see my life flicker by
When I begin to cry
On the dark and
Misty playground.

But here comes the sun
Beaming in my eyes
On the bright and
Glorious playground.

Kimberly Brown (11)
Little Sutton Primary School

Life Doesn't Frighten Me

Spooky spiders, ghostly webs,
Crawling on eight hairy legs,
Life doesn't frighten me at all.
Hooded vampires, dripping fangs,
All alone with endless bangs,
Life doesn't frighten me at all.

Wicked witches on dusty brooms,
Mummies loose outside their tombs,
Life doesn't frighten me at all.
Big black dogs barking loud,
Ice cubes falling from a cloud,
Life doesn't frighten me at all.

I go *no!*
So they go
I'm not shy,
So they cry
I just stand,
Tall and grand
Life doesn't frighten me at all.

Life doesn't frighten me at all
Not hissing cats,
Or barmy bats,
Nor thieving rats, no,
Life doesn't frighten me at all.

Caroline Jeffery (10)
Little Sutton Primary School

Life Doesn't Frighten Me

Aching broken bones,
Gruesome garden gnomes,
Life doesn't frighten me at all.
Dad's pongy feet,
The hole underneath the toilet seat,
Life doesn't frighten me at all.

Terrifying heights,
Pink tutus and tights
Life doesn't frighten me at all.
Sleeping in the dark,
Screaming in the park
Life doesn't frighten me at all.

I scream *go*
They bow low
I forget they are there
They start having a mare
I don't groan
So they moan
Life doesn't frighten me at all.

Giant pirate ships,
Girls' sissy lips,
Life doesn't frighten me at all.
Tied to the train track,
My friend's hairy back,
Life doesn't frighten me at all.

Life doesn't frighten me at all
Not at all
Not at all, not at all
Life doesn't frighten me at all.

Jonathan Lane (10)
Little Sutton Primary School

Life Doesn't Frighten Me At All

Spiders creep me out,
I can't help but shout,
Life doesn't frighten me at all.
Snakes creeping around the room,
Cars giving off a nasty fume,
Life doesn't frighten me at all.

Ghosts calling from all around,
Bodies coming up from underground,
Life doesn't frighten me at all.
People giving you dirty looks,
Being run over by mighty trucks,
Life doesn't frighten me at all.

I go *rah*
They run far,
I'm having fun,
Look at them run,
I won't sob,
I just grin,
Life doesn't frighten me at all.

A lot of people often smoke,
I'd enjoy giving them a hard poke,
Life doesn't frighten me at all.
All of the boys are always mean,
Most of them are anything but clean,
Life doesn't frighten me at all.

Life doesn't frighten me at all
Not at all
Not at all
Life doesn't frighten me at all.

Josie Rea-Miotto (10)
Little Sutton Primary School

The Bully

Some children think a playground is all fun and games,
But when someone gets hurt you'll know who to blame,
The bully!
The bully is tough and really, really rough,
He's very strong but always wrong,
He's the toughest in the year!

When you're playing little clap-song games
Don't forget the bully will always be watching,
But there's no need to fear,
The class superhero will be here to once again save the day.
The bully is on your tail and is bound to make you wail,
The bully is strong and very long,
The bully is big and likes to dig.

The class bully is mean and likes to steal the younger kids' sweets!
But worst of all he trips you over and makes you fall into the
nearest wall.
But tomorrow the bully's leaving and living in Timbuktu
But just be glad that he's moving nowhere near you!

Jessica Nutt (11)
Little Sutton Primary School

Monkey

The monkey swings through the forest,
He's like a ball of fur flying through the sky.
Now he's away from everyone,
Through the trees he goes,
Where is he now? No one knows.
When the monkey comes out to play,
The whole forest becomes alive,
The lions bow down, the tigers stare,
The monkeys gone, the trees now bare.
The monkey looks after his brothers and sisters,
It can be so naughty and so sporty,
The monkey swings through the forest
He's like a ball of fur flying through the sky.

George Lakey (11)
Little Sutton Primary School

There Wasn't A Sound

I walked up the path towards the old dark house.
The door creaked open, and I tiptoed into the cold silent hallway.
There wasn't a sound.

I walked down the corridor, past the mouldy curtains
Mysterious staring faces.
I crept up the broken stairway with damp carpets.
There wasn't a sound.

I peered into the musty bedrooms with moth-eaten mattresses.
I took one frightful look at the musty tin bath in the bathroom.
There wasn't a sound.

I sat on the stairs hoping I'd survive the night.
Something moved behind me. I ran down the stairs.
I felt the floor give way, I fell down, down, down.
There wasn't a sound.
But complete silence.

Grace Chapman (11)
Little Sutton Primary School

Teachers

Some teachers are smart,
Some teachers are dumb,
But guess what!
They all can count up to number one.

Some wear glasses,
That hang in their nose,
Some look down at you,
When you make fun of their toes.

Some are rationale,
Some are fashionable,
But guess what!
They all love to play basketball.

Raenia Soyannwo (11)
Little Sutton Primary School

The Blue Public Transport Bus

He's as blue as day,
But you can't escape,
The blue public transport bus . . .

You will get a fright,
Cos the seatbelts are tight,
In the blue public transport bus . . .

You can jump about,
But you can't get out,
Of the blue public transport bus . . .

The stairs are steep,
Cos they're really cheap,
In the blue public transport bus . . .

He's rarely seen,
He's evil and mean,
Cos he's the blue public transport bus . . .

He's slower than slow,
As public transport goes,
Cos he's an old public transport bus . . .

He will seize you, he will squeeze you!
In a bus that smells just like cheese. *Phew!*
He's the blue . . . the blue . . . public transport bus!

Guy Rogers (11)
Little Sutton Primary School

War Poem

Up ahead the defences stand,
Aimed on every inch of land,
The Germans, man them, ready to kill,
Standing behind them silent and still.

We are here to kill them all,
But looking at them makes us look small.
With a crash our lander hits the beach,
Ahead lies the wall that we must breach.

Beside us our battleships begin to fire,
Fortunately for us they will never tire.
A huge explosion loads of smoke,
The smell of burning, we begin to choke.

We charge forward as the Germans let rip,
All around me friends stumble and trip.
Then I realise that they have been shot,
Blood comes out of them in a big clot.

All around me men are dying,
Many lying on the floor crying.
Four battleships have already been sunk,
A hit on my helmet, another huge clunk.

Soon it will be my turn, my turn to die
I never had a chance to say goodbye.

James Huskisson (11)
Little Sutton Primary School

Life Doesn't Frighten Me

Dogs barking loud
Noises from the clouds
Life doesn't frighten me at all.
Ghosts in your room
Like the man in the moon
Life doesn't frighten me at all.

I go *moo*
So they flew
I just laughed
So they crashed
I shout *Mum*
So they run
I just smirk
So they work.

Life doesn't' frighten me at all
Mean Cruella DeVille
Monsters in the mill
Life doesn't frighten me at all.
Clowns at a fair
Just like a bear
Life doesn't frighten me at all.

Life doesn't frighten me at all
Not at all
Not at all
Life doesn't frighten me at all.

Martyn Ludlow (9)
Little Sutton Primary School

The Graveyard

A scary place
Dating back to the mace
Where the dead sleep
And families weep
They meet at night
And give people a fright
Of course I'm talking about a graveyard
It's not like a backyard
It's waking up to a ghost on a Monday morning
'Cause you are mourning
Scared at night
My! What a fright!
The rain bangs down on most days
The price to pay is a heavy one
Wind breathing
Thunder clattering
Clouds booming
Rain pattering
Lightning crashing
Tombstones shattering
Of course, it's a sad day in a graveyard.

Julia Barbour (10)
Little Sutton Primary School

Untitled

I'm a monkey
I create mischief.
I am quite sporty
Yet I'm very, very naughty.

I am a lion,
King of the jungle.
I'll let out a roar that'll
Shake the floor.

I am a parrot,
I'm bright orange like a carrot.
I squawk and squeak
With my sharp beak.

We are animals
We own the jungle.
We keep ourselves to ourselves.
We know our place on the shelf
And so should you too.

Marcus Rowbotham (11)
Little Sutton Primary School

Teachers

Some teachers are ugly
Some teachers are pretty
But all I know is . . .
My teacher is the best.

Some teachers are nice
Some teachers are mean
But all I know is . . .
They are not all they seem.

Some teachers are boring
Some teachers are fun
But all I know is . . .
They love pink iced buns.

Jessica Hipkiss (11)
Little Sutton Primary School

Everything I'm Scared Of

Shadows all around,
Ghosts making sounds,
Life doesn't frighten me at all.
All the doors are creaking,
Monsters speaking,
Life doesn't frighten me at all.

Creatures under the bed,
I heard the things they said,
Life doesn't frighten me at all.
Tough guys wanting to kill,
All of a sudden everything still,
Life doesn't frighten me at all.

I stand proud,
In a crowd,
I pull faces,
In the races,
Clowns go *boo,*
I say *shoo,*
Life doesn't frighten me at all.

The ghost of the classroom moving slow,
Wanting all of us to go,
Life doesn't frighten me at all.
The black hole sucking up,
People say I'm out of luck,
Life doesn't frighten me at all.

Life doesn't frighten me at all,
Not at all,
Not at all,
Life doesn't frighten me at all.

Natasha Cope (10)
Little Sutton Primary School

Life Doesn't Frighten Me At All

Snakes all around,
Spiders on the ground,
Life doesn't frighten me at all.
Sleeping in the dark,
Dogs in the park,
Life doesn't frighten me at all.

Monsters under the bed having a meal,
I wish they weren't real,
Life doesn't frighten me at all.
Injections giving me a fright,
Panthers in the park,
Life doesn't frighten me at all.

I stand tall,
They go small,
I think very smart,
They do scary art,
Life doesn't frighten me at all.

Shivers down my spine,
Making them feel fine,
Life doesn't frighten me at all.
Spooks on the wall,
Noises down the hall,
Life doesn't frighten me at all.

Life doesn't frighten me at all,
Not at all,
Not at all,
Life doesn't frighten me at all.

Bethany Lea-Redmond (10)
Little Sutton Primary School

Life Doesn't Frighten Me At All!

Elevators stopping still,
People wanting to kill,
Life doesn't frighten me at all.
Fearsome dogs in the park,
Spiteful strangers in the dark,
Life doesn't frighten me at all.

Spooky ghosts going through the wall,
Long slippery snakes eating things small,
Life doesn't frighten me at all.
Army men in a battle of war,
Hairy spiders creeping under the door,
Life doesn't frighten me at all.

I go *boo,*
They get the flu,
I stand tall,
They go small,
I go *raaa,*
They run far,
Life doesn't frighten me at all.

Roaring lions always eating meat,
Silly people always wanting to cheat,
Life doesn't frighten me at all.
Thundering lightning, it's all bad weather,
Scary-looking people, millions of leather,
Life doesn't frighten me at all.

Life doesn't frighten me at all,
Not at all,
Not at all,
Life doesn't frighten me at all!

Louka Nicodemou (10)
Little Sutton Primary School

Life Doesn't Frighten Me At All

Dark, dark, dark,
Monsters in the park,
Life doesn't frighten me at all.
Thunder and lightning,
Really very frightening,
Life doesn't frighten me at all.

Big steep stairs,
But I don't care,
Life doesn't frighten me at all.
Big dogs and their big teeth,
But I just ignore them and pick up a leaf,
Life doesn't frighten me at all.

I go *rah,*
They say *tah,*
I'm having fun,
They just run,
I just grin,
They hide in bins,
Life doesn't frighten me at all.

Wandering around,
Not a sound,
Life doesn't frighten me at all.
Violent vacuum,
Going vroom, vroom, vroom,
Life doesn't frighten me at all.

Life doesn't frighten me at all,
Not at all,
Not at all,
Life doesn't frighten me at all.

Becky Richards (10)
Little Sutton Primary School

Life Doesn't Frighten Me At All

Hairy spiders down the hall,
Big cats climbing up the wall,
Life doesn't frighten me at all.
Toilet flushing
My mom blushing,
Life doesn't frighten me at all.

Ghosts disguised up in the air,
Little creepy-crawlies in my hair,
Life doesn't frighten me at all.
Monsters in the park,
Bats in the dark
Life doesn't frighten me at all.

I go *roar*
Make them snore,
I'm all alone
But I don't moan,
Life doesn't frighten me at all.

Wolves blowing down houses,
While cats are eating mouses,
Life doesn't frighten me at all.
Talking computers beeping,
While I'm sleeping,
Life doesn't frighten me at all.

Life doesn't frighten me at all,
Not at all, not at all,
Life doesn't frighten me at all.

Gemma Shepherd (10)
Little Sutton Primary School

Battle!

Bazooka in my hand as I'm standing here,
My stomach is hurting, crawling with fear,
I am squelching on the wet, black sand
Standing here, bazooka in my hand.

I'm petrified, away from home
Forget about that, I'm here alone!
I left my family, I regret it now
If I could go back I would . . . somehow.

My mortar blasting people to Hell,
The shotgun doing the same as well.
Bang! Bang! I'm shot in the head,
I'm slowly dying, dying, dead.

With my last ounce of strength,
I fall on the ground,
Saying goodbye to the weapons I've found,
I can't believe that I'm going to die
Without saying to my family the simple words 'Goodbye.'

William Banks (10)
Little Sutton Primary School

Birds Of Prey

Seeking for food,
The falcon glares with his regal eyes
Scanning the cold, autumnal mountains, wolves howling,
There it is . . . it's a rabbit!
Gliding down the majestic valley,
The barbed claws sink into the victim,
The pain, the agony of pierced flesh,
Pecking, pinching, and ripping into the meaty defenceless creature.
This falcon ready for nightfall, circles over the nests of hare,
He sees more food and the adventures of the golden falcon continue.

Todd Millward (11)
Mount Pleasant Primary School

Bird Of Prey

An eagle springing toward a craggy, rocky mountain fence
Plummets, drops, as an eagle dives

Eagles gliding swiftly in an azure world
Eagles can spot a rabbit bouncing in the grass
Then the eagle swooped down
Watching the rabbit like a hawk circling around the rabbit.
Eagles have silent flights at night.

Ryan Fellows (9)
Mount Pleasant Primary School

Owl

Owls swooping outside
I think to myself, I want an owl like that.
Owls beautifully feathered, I can see their beautiful green eyes.
Owls outside like a melt-water splashed in a puddle of mud.
Their claws are dangerous like a wolf eating meat.
So you better watch out.
Now it has gone I have to go to bed.
Goodnight owl, I hope you come again another night.

Bethany Wilkins (10)
Mount Pleasant Primary School

Owl

An amazing owl
Gliding through the sky
They have amber searchlights to see.
Owls are perfect they can eat in one mouthful
They go out at night and look for their food.
Silent night have a lovely night!

Hayley Whyte (10)
Mount Pleasant Primary School

A Circus Poem

It is circus day
So let's go out and play

Lots of people playing around
Some standing, some on the ground

Look at these children there is a lot
I bet they are really hot

It is time, it is time
Quick everyone get in line

Some people spinning plates
Some people lifting weights

Oh no, today has ended
My happiness has faded.

Bethany Smith (10)
Mount Pleasant Primary School

The Owl Frogget

As Frogget swoops down
His feathers flow with him gently.

His eyes glow like amber searchlights
In the dusk!

As he reaches the azure world
He camouflages so no one can see him.

He grabs his meaty prey
With his sharp talons.

When he's finished he starts
His silent fight again.

Gemma Raybould (10)
Mount Pleasant Primary School

The Owl

His name is Frogget
And he swoops through the air.

He is silent
His prey can't hear him
Until he pounces.

His amber searchlight eyes
Search for prey and predators.

He calls out
Who? Who? Who?
As he plummets to the ground.

When he seizes his prey
His talons squeeze them
To their untimely death.

Sam Freestone (10)
Mount Pleasant Primary School

Feed The World!

People dying, people crying,
Feed the world,
Tents flapping, children starving,
Feed the world.

No rain, people dehydrated,
Feed the world,
Refugees fleeting, no hope,
Feed the world.

When I finished that poem
Five people died in Africa,
So please, please feed the world.

Anthony Thomas (11)
Mount Pleasant Primary School

A Day At The Circus

It's circus time
Hip hip hooray! I wonder what I'll see today?
Shall I go on this ride
Or eat in a café?
Perhaps I'll ride on a giraffe
I'm feeling hungry
What shall I have?
Doughnuts and cream
Or go to the candyfloss man?
I'm having a lovely time at the circus
Today I'll go on the rides
Whee hip hooray!
It's time for a show
What will it be, eh?
It's an elephant coming to me
'Hello,' I say and then we go
It's getting late
So I will leave
A lovely time at the circus
I believe.

Katie-Jo Clarke (10)
Mount Pleasant Primary School

Dolphins

Dolphins, dolphins,
Swimming through the ocean,
Dipping and diving
Through the deep waves.
Speaking to their friends,
Dancing like a ballerina,
Magical, mysterious,
King of the ocean.

How I wish I were you.

Sophie Round (7)
Mount Pleasant Primary School

The Owl

I sleep all through the day,
And awake in the night,
I listen for movement,
Just the rustling of leaves will do,
Crack.
The crack of a twig,
Just half a mile off,
I shall leave my nest,
But when I return my chicks shall have food.

I glide away from my nest,
But closer to my prey,
My feathers give me silent flight,
I twist my head around slowly,
To get a sight of my prey,
My ebony eyes spot a young rabbit,
Manoeuvring in-between the undergrowth,
My eyes lock onto my prey,
I dive down through the trees,
And my claws seize the unsuspecting rabbit.

I soar back up into the air
The moon creates a shadow of my wings,
On the overgrown forest floor,
I dive back down into my nest,
And feed my young,
Now I am ready to do the same again,
Tomorrow night.

Matthew Round (10)
Mount Pleasant Primary School

Eagle

Eagle sitting on a sea-smoothed rock,
Surveying the area for a sign of life,
Suddenly his head darts to the river,
Wasting no time at all he lifts his wings and takes off,
Soaring through the air birds scatter, mice scarper,
Curling his talons to strike,
The sound of death spreads for miles,
Stuck to his feet another victim loses their life.

Landing back on the rock,
Eagle scans the area again,
The sound of ripping,
Now eagle sits on a blood-red stone,
Marking clearly,
Showing the world,
This is his territory,
Find your own.

Matthew Simmonds (10)
Mount Pleasant Primary School

Owl

The owl awakens in the dead of the night
Ready to engage in silent fight
Up and up he flies with amber headlight eyes
This bird of prey, surely mortifies
All creatures who stand against him
Will after regret this sorrow within
Whilst the hills are bandaged in darkness
The owl flies the farthest
For when the owl returns home
He stays on his branch, as still as stone
Now that the owl has finished his duty
He remains at rest, with regal beauty.

Adam Lambe (9)
Mount Pleasant Primary School

Who Cares?

Crying, drying,
Family all gone,
One by one - they suffer.
Rice at a price,
Can't afford it now.
No one can - we are all dying.
Dead,
Drop dead . . .
Who cares?

Starving,
No one cares!
Children in Ethiopia aren't any better off.
What are we?
Useless!
No clean water to drink beneath our swollen lips.
People die all around me.
I'm next!
Dead,
Drop dead.

Who cares?

Six children died in Africa whilst you read this . . . think!

Katie North (11)
Mount Pleasant Primary School

Froggett

Froggett swoops down from high mountains
With his long, ruffled feathers out wide beside him.

As soon as he touches the floor
His long talons grab onto his prey.

Once he has finished his prey he stands still
Like a statue
And dives again
With a silent flight!

Charlie Heaton (9)
Mount Pleasant Primary School

Clown Or Creeper

The blasphemous clown crept silently,
Plotting a diabolical plan behind his blood-red gash.
His overgrown mossy eyebrows make him sinful and his pitch-black
Abhorrent eyes watch his audience of screaming children.
The baggy clothes he wears hide his evilness and his real self.
His fluorescent orange shock of hair leaps out
Of his nearly bald head in tufts.
The tone of his sacrilegious face is unpleasant and forbidding.
No one laughs at this cunning criminal clown as he is not funny, but
peculiar and menacing!
His entertainment is corrupt and hair-raising.
He makes a child's party worse than dreadful.
His gaudy face is icy cold and he has spidery eyelashes.
His loathsome personality is vile and unworthy.
No one thinks much of this cruel clown, hidden in rotten paints.
His breath gives a macabre feeling to the air.
Children dislike his fixed smile and devilish arches
That crown his vicious eyes.
He is villainous, bloodthirsty and barbaric.

Georgia Williams (11)
Mount Pleasant Primary School

The Clown

A sinister looking clown silently stepped into the ring,
A sly smile and ghoulish eyes all painted with black paint,
Everybody loves clowns, but not this one,
His haunted face and matted hair made everybody turn away.
His devilish thick arches for eyebrows painted in black
And his icy white face make him look like a ghost.
He is not a good clown to meet although he has funny clothes
But in black and white, his nose is all blood red and stuffy,
A bowler hat, black with no flower,
What a wicked looking clown.

Leah Bangham (10)
Mount Pleasant Primary School

The Magic Box

(Based on 'Magic Box' by Kit Wright)

I will put in my box . . .
The first swish of a lion's mane
The miaow of a baby kitten
The squeak of a dormouse.

I will put in my box . . .
A spark from an electric eel
A perfect, purple poppy
A beautiful, blue butterfly.

I will put in my box . . .
The smell of a sweet turquoise tulip
The aroma of a beautiful perfume
The scent of honey from a bear's paw.

I will put in my box . . .
The smooth touch of a kitten's paw
The soft silk of an English spaniel's ear
The roughness of a porcupine's back.

My box is fashioned from many precious gems and diamonds
From dark gold mines with precious stars around its edge
And elephant tusk hinges.

I shall climb into the box and go to Mars, Milky Way
And around the Galaxy.

Georgia Fitzsimmons (7)
Mount Pleasant Primary School

Owls

Owls flying through the air swiftly and softly.
Owls swiftly glide through the invisible sparkling air.
Owls have bright lights through the night lights!
Owls swiftly glide through the invisible sparkling air.
Owls have bright lights shining through the night lights!

Jack Brookes (10)
Mount Pleasant Primary School

Crying, Lying, Dying

Crying, lying, dying,
Some are having food,
Some are craving food,
Fresh water,
Dirty water.

Crying, lying, dying,
Some have clothes,
Some do not,
Rain,
No rain.

Crying, lying, dying,
Some have houses,
Some are looking,
Rich,
Poor.

Tiffany Johnstone (10)
Mount Pleasant Primary School

The Circus

In the circus I can see
Acrobats acting like a seal.

In the circus I can smell
A quarter-pounder burger cooking really well.

In the circus I can see
These seats starting to peel.

In the circus I can taste
This chocolate bar with a lot of paste.

In the circus I can hear
Lots of people starting to fear.

Daniel Pearson (9)
Mount Pleasant Primary School

The Seasons

January brings the snow,
Everybody says, 'Oh No!'

February brings the rain,
We all hurry down the wet lane.

March brings breezes loud and shrill,
We all have to pay our electric bill!

April brings the primrose sweet,
The grassy fields tickle our feet.

May brings flocks of pretty lambs,
All playing with their mother dams.

June brings tulips, lilies and roses,
With lots of pretty flower posies.

Hot July brings cooling showers,
All animals use their charming powers.

August brings the sheaves of corn,
Some of us love the warm.

Warm September brings happy days,
Everybody goes outside and plays.

October brings the dark nights,
People struggle to see the lights.

November brings the winter chill,
Everybody stays warm and still.

December brings the Christmas cheer,
Santa Claus is nearly here.

Ella Morgan (7)
Mount Pleasant Primary School

The Magic Box

(Based on 'Magic Box' by Kit Wright)

I will put in my box . . .
The sweetest quack of a duck
The swish of a stupendous smelling breeze
The merry buzzing of a bumble bee.

I will put in my box . . .
A special spark of a flaming firework
The magnificent models from a fashion show
A perfect pyramid that crumbles.

I will put in my box . . .
The smell of a rumbling roast dinner
The scent of a butterfly on a flower
The smell of a thousand little bubbles.

I will put in my box . . .
A tiny drop of a tear
A pearl from my face
The feel of honey on my skin.

I will put in my box . . .
The feel of a lion's mane
A piece of shiny curly hair
The feel of a precious petal.

My box is fashioned from lovely luscious silk from a foreign land
A wave from the bluest ocean
And a crash of lightning bolt is on its lid
Its hinges are the delicate shells from the sea.

I shall go to the stars and dance with the starlings way above Earth
With my box for company.

Abigail Homer (8)
Mount Pleasant Primary School

Fireworks

Fireworks, fireworks bang and boom,
Heading straight for the moon.

In the darkness comes bright light,
From the fireworks burning light.

Right in the sky they fly so high,
Enormous colours scatter the sky.

Everywhere they fly around,
As we look from on the ground.

'Wow!' Shout the children as they go by,
'Look at the fireworks in the sky.'

Only light from the moon,
Hope it doesn't end too soon.

Right away they shoot up high,
Almost seeming to fly.

King of the skies the fireworks fly,
Twirling, swirling, hope they never die.

Reece Bourne (8)
Mount Pleasant Primary School

Owl

Eyes like to search through the sky.
Ruffled feathers fly through the night.
Fur, black as ebony, plotting for prey.
Claws seize and squeeze prey.

The owl, diving in at the speed of light, seizes its prey.
The owl seizes and squeezes its prey
And carries it off to its babies.

Jack Green (10)
Mount Pleasant Primary School

The Leopard

T he leopard hunts all through daylight,
H e eats all day and rests at night,
E ating all types of jungle treats.

L eopard, leopard his eyes gleam yellow,
E xercising through the magical forest,
O nly he is king of his land,
P rowling like a spider in its web,
A re you daring to face him?
R emember he runs like lightning,
D readed hunter, that's him.

Adam Lowe (8)
Mount Pleasant Primary School

Elephants

E xcellent elephants prancing around.
L eaping through the jungle ground.
E verywhere inside the wonderful wood.
P rancing around like they should.
H eavy footsteps all around.
A nts are delicious, found on the ground.
N oisy stomping of a herd.
T rumpeting cry scares each bird.

Scott Smith (8)
Mount Pleasant Primary School

Spring

S unny days are coming fast,
P lants are growing with new flowers,
R ain is coming to life
I see new buds growing
N ew season is coming
G reen roots are being born.

Lucy Baker (7)
Mount Pleasant Primary School

The Clowns

As you walk behind the red curtains
You wonder what is there
You go in and you sit down
Sit back and enjoy the show
You see acrobats sweeping through the air
And jugglers with seven balls and flying flags
Clowns falling and wooden stilts
The clowns are falling off their unicycles
And throwing pies at each other.

Jordan Debra-Washington (10)
Mount Pleasant Primary School

Dinner Time For Owl

Owl's eyes beam like light
As owl glides, her feathers ruffle
No other animal can see owl
She's in camouflage
As soon as owl sees food
She flies down
Squeezes her claws together
And eats it in darkness.

Danielle Baker (10)
Mount Pleasant Primary School

Eagle Eyes

Eyes like amber searchlights
Glowing in the midnight sky,
Catching sheep from large fields,
Taking them to remote places
And squeezing them to death,
Going back to the field and collecting mice and voles
Taking them back to the nest,
And this is where the night ends.

Andrew Raybould (9)
Mount Pleasant Primary School

Comet

The blazing rock
The fiery furnace
The iris blaze
The mysterious rock
The speeding flames
The blazing furnace
The iris trail
The speeding rock
The plummeting rock
The mysterious trail
The blazing flames
The blazing oven
The plummeting oven
The blazing barbeque
The flaming chilli
The overheated oven
The speeding rock
The blazing chilli
The speeding rock
The blazing chilli
The speeding barbeque
The plummeting furnace
The overheated chilli
The plummeting trail.

Aaran Tranter (9)
Mount Pleasant Primary School

Owls

Owls are very fast as they glide through the sky.
Owls can see at night as they squeeze their prey.
Their eyes are like amber searchlights in the darkness.
Ruffled feathers as they glide through the night.
Owls fly silently in the sky.

Rio Wood (10)
Mount Pleasant Primary School

Owl

He plummets from the tallest of trees
To seize his prey
With his razor-sharp talons.
He glides down like a jet
In total silence
To claim his snack.
He watches slowly and
Twists his head in curiosity
Hoping to find
Another snack.

Matthew Jones (10)
Mount Pleasant Primary School

The Owl

Ruffled, soft feathers
Camouflaged in the ebony sky.
Eyes like amber searchlights
Look for their prey.
Claws like lion's hands
Ready to seize and squeeze.
Wings so strong to hold him up high
As he flies his silent flight.

Laura Whitehead (9)
Mount Pleasant Primary School

Butterflies

In the spring wings are colourful and bright,
Fluttering and flying all around.
Playing in and out of the flowers,
Silent singing of their song,
Multicoloured patterns,
Darting rainbows.

Emily Leipacher (7)
Mount Pleasant Primary School

The Eagle

As I look into the night sky,
I seem to spy an elegant eagle.
His wings spread out far,
Searching for night-time prey,
But nothing so far.

All of a sudden, like a lightning bolt,
He darts to the floor.
But yet again you see a swoop to the sky,
He's returning to his perch,
Up high on a crag.

Daniel Layland (9)
Mount Pleasant Primary School

Owl

Grey is his colour
Torches are his eyes
He seeks the creature and shoots
Down like a bullet being shot out of a pistol
He pulls out his daggers and stabs them into the creature
He then munches down on his snack
The winds blow, which ruffles up his feathers
This wonderful creature is Owl.

Melvyn Mathews (9)
Mount Pleasant Primary School

The Hawk

Night-time searches are the best,
As the fierce creature rests upon a rusty lamp post.

The hawk's eyes are like amber searchlights,
Glaring down at his juicy prey.

The hawk's talons are ready to snatch,
As he swoops down to seize and squeeze.

Olivia Fullwood (10)
Mount Pleasant Primary School

The Owl

As the owl sits in his nest his eyes are
As quick as lightning, looking after his prey.
He camouflaged himself so he does not scare away anything.
His eyes like amber searchlights
Glowing in the dark, in the swaying, damp grass.
He glides through the air,
Gets out his razor-sharp claws,
And picks up, sticking in his claws and
That's me done for the night.

Victoria Webb (10)
Mount Pleasant Primary School

Star

The star is bright and it's like a fireball
In the sky at night-time, I stare at it.
It reminds me of fairy godparents in the sky
And lots of power to wish that I was on the star.
But I don't feel like I am on the star
I want the power of the star
Now so I can be a star in the sky
And I will make some friends up there now.

Sandeep Patel (9)
Mount Pleasant Primary School

Bees

Bees are nasty, fierce and mean,
They can sting and attack,
Collecting the sweet pollen below,
Making honey from their store,
Buzzing, buzzing, buzzing.
The king of the skies.

James Hampson (6)
Mount Pleasant Primary School

The Man In The Moon

The mysterious man in the moon,
Who are you?
Sitting all night staring down,
Watching the Earth so bright.

The man in the moon is a happy sight,
Gazing at the stars so bright,
What are you thinking?
What do you see?

The man in the moon,
Lights the world up,
Sees everything without making a fuss,
But makes no noise.

Man in the moon,
Who are you?

Lucy Bradley (8)
Mount Pleasant Primary School

The Eagle

His eyes are like amber searchlights,
Black as ebony in the night,
Camouflaged to its prey
Ruffled feathers stand on end,
In silent flight.
The woods are bandaged in darkness,
Swooping down he seizes
And squeezes his prey.
Gracefully flying back to his nest,
With his prey in his mouth and he proudly
Rips his prey apart and eats it.
The eagle owl is the blindfold of death.

Daniel Woodfield (10)
Mount Pleasant Primary School

The Hawk

Eyes like cats
Shining like a sun
Ebony feathers ruffle
Then it dives
From rocky mountains
With a swoop, it catches death
Circling the azure sky
It makes a fierce, breaking squawk
Then it lands, creature fearless.

Louisa Hampson (9)
Mount Pleasant Primary School

Butterflies

Butterflies flying in the wind
Chasing the bees,
Zooming across houses,
Peeping in doors,
Whizzing and twirling,
Gliding and falling,
Landing on petals,
Dancing in the air.

Estelle Pedley (7)
Mount Pleasant Primary School

Dragons

Dragons, dragons believe in them,
Roaring, racing around the world,
'Ah!' The raging dragons roar.
Great at fighting everyone
Only find them hiding away
Never see them in the light of day
Scary and fierce creatures.

Chandler Massey (7)
Mount Pleasant Primary School

Owls

Owls fly
Owls glide
Owls swoop
Owls shoot into the sky.

Owls squawk
Owls screech
Owls catch
Owls blink
Owls leap into the sky.

Owls, owls
Owls squeak
Like a rocket in the sky
And owls shoot up and down and even
Glide up and down.

Owls shoot down like a shooting star
And they also glide softly in the sky.

Thomas Taylor (9)
Mount Pleasant Primary School

Football

F ootball's crazy
O wen hat tricks
O ver the world
T he match begins
B end it like Beckham
A super header
L ovely shot by Shaun Wright-Phillips
L uscious volley by Rooney.

C razy saves
R ooney rages
A wesome defence
Z ooming balls
Y ou win the game!

Nathan Greenwood (8)
Mount Pleasant Primary School

The Birthday Clown

A clown came to my birthday once
How dreadful he became,
His aim - to spoil my birthday
Like his was once abolished.

The evil rap had an everlasting echo, banging on the door,
Its shadow blocked out the sun,
It looked like night had fallen,
That piercing glare,
The unyielding walk,
As deadly as they come.

I'll always remember,
The third of September
A sight I'll never forget,
The interminable synthetic smile
The gaudy avalanche of hair,
Overgrown rushes as eyebrows
Surrounded two murky swamps
A grotesque black growth in place of a human nose.
He popped the balloons,
And ripped my birthday banner,
As he walked out the door,
He'd done as he swore,
He ruined my birthday party!

Bradley Saunders (10)
Mount Pleasant Primary School

Dragons

Dragons are ferocious
Dragons are scary
They have beady eyes
And they will eat you for supper
So see if you find
A dragon like me
You do follow me to destiny!

Ellouise Banks (8)
Mount Pleasant Primary School

A Sinister Clown

Moulting and drooped,
Curls uncurling,
The wig is beginning to look like a rat's nest,
Eyebrows are like thin crowns leading to black holes.

The mask of the unknown
Mysterious
Ghoulish
Ha, ha, ha,
Who is the sinister clown?

Cats eyes look like ovals with daggers pierced through.
Long, spidery legs are tickling cheeks from below black holes.
Ears as pointed as a mountain peak,
Noses the colour of a blood blister.

The mask of the unknown,
Mysterious, ghoulish,
Ha, ha, ha,
What is the sinister clown?

A dead half moon, lying on its side,
Sharp fangs emerging from it
A goatie-like beard, grey and smudgy.

The mask of the unknown,
Mysterious, ghoulish,
Ha, ha, ha,
Where is the sinister clown?

Facial colours are just white,
Facial features are just black,
An ebony cloak hides the truth.

The mask of the unknown.
Mysterious, ghoulish,
Ha, ha, ha.
I am the sinister
Clown!

Bethany Madkins (11)
Mount Pleasant Primary School

The Clown

He appeared out of the ebony darkness,
Everyone went deadly silent.
Gazing intently, he looked at all the shocked faces,
Until he stopped and stared at one certain person.
His face was icy cold, white figure swaying from side to side.
Everyone eagerly fixed their eyes on his ethereal, spectral face.
Spidery thin hairs descended from his beady eyes.
Those hairs gave him a grotesque look.
From his head came an avalanche of sickly-coloured hair.
Whilst curls matted from his sweaty, dirty wig.
Fiendish crowns rested above his head
Or you could say they were great arches.
A sad smile turned into a fixed grimace,
It soon turned back to an unhappy blood-red gash.
His beady eyes filled the room with eternal darkness.
Closing his diabolical eyes,
He descended into the pitch-black shadows to hide his figure.
There was not a trace of sound,
It was like he wasn't there . . . !

Brandan Slater (10)
Mount Pleasant Primary School

My Friends

One of my friends is extremely tall,
Her head touches the ceiling in the hall!

One of my friends is extremely happy,
But her baby sister needs some nappies!

Some of my friends always fall out,
But they always like to scream and shout!

My special friend lives near the sea,
And he really does adore me!

But best of all I have to say,
My best of all friends is Molly May!

Rebecca Bradley (7)
Mount Pleasant Primary School

Clown

As he walks down the street
Staring around everywhere,
Creeping daintily
Shock of hair rustling as loud as the leaves
Like a rat's nest
Sprouts of hair everywhere,
Leering wickedly
Balls of midnight madness.

Sickly-coloured,
Intimidating,
Soulless as a book,
Mysterious, shadowy, dark ebony eyes,
Bizarre, freaky
He is as cold as ice.
Feeling lonely, left out.
Muscular, fantastic
Superb at juggling,
Eyelashes as big as his eyes,
Mouth as big as an elastic band,
Sneering sinisterly,
Being a worn-out clown
Raggy hair, like feather dusters,
Wants to have friends.

Daniel Appleton (10)
Mount Pleasant Primary School

Springtime

In the spring, trees all sway in the golden sun.
Bunnies jump happily along, finding food to eat
So they can go to sleep.
Baby lambs just been born,
Running happily along.
Easter Bunny, searching for eggs,
A very special time of year.
The end of winter; a new beginning.

Abby Byrne (8)
Mount Pleasant Primary School

Dreams

In the night I go to sleep.
It's dark, it's quiet, I'm having a dream.
The light is off.
The door is closed.
The windows are shut.
It's cold, eerie.
It's raining outside.
I listen to the pitter-patter on the rooftops.
Suddenly, my dreams take over.
My mind starts to wander.
Images running through my mind.
Twirling, swirling through my brain.
My eyes start to flicker.
My body awakes.
My dream is over.
Night-time sleeps.
Morning awakes.

Katie Whitehead (7)
Mount Pleasant Primary School

Feed The World

Dying of famine
Children are dying
Bodies are weak
Dehydrated bodies
Children have rumbling bellies
Please help the poor children
Babies are ill, please help
Flies around the baby
Feed the world
World needs food.

Rikesh Patel (10)
Mount Pleasant Primary School

Fireworks

Fireworks, fireworks
Flying around and around.

Fireworks, fireworks
Spinning to the ground.

Fireworks, fireworks,
Whizzing and fizzing.

Fireworks, fireworks
On the 5th of November . . . remember!

Fireworks, fireworks,
Racing and chasing.

Fireworks, fireworks
A night to remember.

Crashing, fizzing,
Chasing and racing . . .
A fun time for all.

Daniel Turley (8)
Mount Pleasant Primary School

Jaguar

Jaguar, jaguar - a hunting machine,
Jaguar, jaguar - jumping through the trees.
Jaguar, jaguar - hunting its prey.
Jaguar, jaguar - scratching all day.
Jaguar, jaguar - killing its prey.
Jaguar, jaguar - running away.
Jaguar, jaguar - not too close.
Jaguar, jaguar - braver than most.
Jaguar, jaguar - ready to bite.
Watch out because he's ready to fight.

Rory King (7)
Mount Pleasant Primary School

Bonfire

B rilliant fireworks
O range, fiery sky
N ight to remember
F antastic sight
I ncredible fun
R oaring of the fire
E ventually ends.

Alex Sambidge (8)
Mount Pleasant Primary School

Happy

Happy is yellow like a sunny day.
It's like a bird singing in the tree.
It feels like a soft pillow.
It reminds me of lots of nice flowers.
Happy is a smile.
When you smile you pass it on forever and ever.
Smile forever and ever.

Ameera Moore (8)
New Oscott Junior School

Happiness

Happiness is like a red arrow drawing five kisses,
It reminds me of a lorry painting a picture of a lady,
It looks like a little girl smiling.
It sounds like a lady singing in the sunny garden.
It tastes like a red cherry and they are very sweet too.
It feels like a red wave drowning me on the beach.
It smells like a red volcano burning me to pieces.

Emma Jeeves (8)
New Oscott Junior School

Fear

Fear is scary like aliens.
It's really scary.
It is really scary.
It looks like darkness in the shadow.
It reminds me of my angry brother.

Ryan Ledward (8)
New Oscott Junior School

Bullying Cinquain

Spiteful,
A bully is,
Horrible, cruel, nasty,
They kick you and punch you a lot,
Stop it!

They will
Hurt your feelings,
Uncooperative,
You feel you don't want to be here,
Speak up!

Nasty,
Stand up, speak up,
They think it's really cool,
They show off in front of their mates,
Oh please!

They're vile,
They swear at you,
They hurt you really bad,
And this means, he is a bully.
Coward!

Rebecca Booth (10)
Rough Hay Primary School

Bullying Cinquains

Spiteful,
A bully is,
Punching, hitting, hurting,
Also a bully is nasty,
Stop it!

Nasty,
A bully is,
Cheeky, lonely, unkind,
Some bullies think they are so cool,
Please stop!

Laughing,
A bully is,
Moaning at each other,
Also bullies don't care too much,
Stop now!

Chloè Richards (11)
Rough Hay Primary School

Bullying Cinquains

Break time,
A bully is,
Horrible, nasty, cruel,
They kick you and punch you a lot.
Stop it!

They will,
Hurt your feelings,
Uncooperative,
You feel you don't want to be here.
Speak up!

Nasty,
Stand up, speak up,
They think it's really cool,
They show off in front of their mates.
Coward!

Brandon Maxfield (11)
Rough Hay Primary School

Bullying

Spiteful
A bully is,
Punching, hitting, hurting,
Also a bully is naughty.
Stop it!

Nasty,
A bully is,
Cheeky, lonely, unkind,
Some bullies think they are so cool.
Please stop!

Laughing,
A bully is,
Laughing at each other,
Also bullies can't care much.
Stop now!

Not nice
Not nice at all because
They hit anybody in their sight.
Now stop!

Joseph Evans (11)
Rough Hay Primary School

Bullying

B eat bullying,
U ncaring bullies,
L earn your lesson,
L eave me alone,
Y ou are spiteful,
I nconsiderate bullies,
N ever kind to others,
G *o away you bully!*

Beau Westwood (10)
Rough Hay Primary School

Bullying Cinquains

Spiteful,
A bully is,
Kicking, punching, hurting,
A bully can be nasty too.
Please stop!

Nasty,
A bully is,
Cheeky, spiteful, lonely,
Also a bully is unkind.
Stop it!

Laughing,
At each other,
Don't run by the bullies,
And bullies don't care very much.
Stop now!

Not nice,
A bully is,
Not kind at all because
They hit anybody in sight.
No stop!

Michael Collins (10)
Rough Hay Primary School

Friends

F unky friends,
R ed as a strawberry,
I maginative as a mind,
E xcellent as Mrs Bird,
N ever naughty like a butterfly
D elightful as a lollipop
S uccessful like all the teachers.

Katie Griffiths (10)
Rough Hay Primary School

Bullying Cinquains

Nasty,
You pick on me,
Punching and kicking me,
Please stop! Please stop! Stop now! Please stop!
Stop it!

Spiteful,
You're hurting me,
Slapping me, hitting me,
I am hurting inside, please stop!
No! no!

Laughing,
I am hurting,
My heart is breaking now.
Don't do that! Don't do that ever!
Again!

You go,
I am left here,
No one is helping me!
I am really bloody from you.
Help me!

Jessica Saunders (11)
Rough Hay Primary School

Bullying Cinquains

Spiteful,
Is a bully,
He is so very vile,
Nobody really likes him much.
Not cool!

Jade Webb (11)
Rough Hay Primary School

Bullying Cinquains

Spiteful,
A bully is,
Horrible, nasty, cruel,
They kick you and punch you a lot.
Stop it!

They will,
Hurt your feelings,
Uncooperative,
You feel you don't want to be here.
Speak up!

Nasty,
Stand up, speak up,
They think it's really cool,
They show off in front of their mates.
Oh please!

They're vile,
They swear at you,
They hurt you really bad,
And this means he is a bully.
Coward!

Stephanie Eccleston (11)
Rough Hay Primary School

Bullying Cinquain

I think,
A bully is,
Horrible and nasty,
Nobody likes them much they are
Spiteful.

Matthew Bott (11)
Rough Hay Primary School

Bullying Cinquains

Spiteful,
A bully is,
Punching, hitting, hurting,
Also a bully is harmful.
Stop it!

Nasty,
A bully is,
Cheeky, lonely, unkind,
Some bullies think they are so cool.
Please stop!

Laughing,
A bully is,
Laughing at each other,
And bullies don't care very much.
Stop now!

Not nice,
A bully is,
Not kind at all because
They hit anybody in sight.
Now stop!

Victoria Greenway-Brown (11)
Rough Hay Primary School

Bullying Cinquains

Spiteful,
A bully is,
Half-witted and grumpy,
Nasty, horrible, unkind, hard.
Stop now!

Selfish,
He cheeks my mom,
He cheeks my family,
It makes me very, very sad.
Stop it!

Joshua Talbot (11)
Rough Hay Primary School

Bullying

B eat bullying
U ncaring bullies
L earn your lesson
L eave me alone
Y ou are spiteful
I nconsiderate bullies
N ever kind to each other
G o away!

Kyle Smart (11)
Rough Hay Primary School

Bullying

B ig, bad bully
U nlucky bully
L ow life bully
L onely bully
Y elling bully
I gnorant, idle bully
N asty bully
G rumpy bully.

Damien Crammond (11)
Rough Hay Primary School

Bullying

B adly behaved bully
U tterly unkind bully
L oud, lonely bully
L ow, lying bully
Y elling, youthful bully
I gnorant, idle bully
N aughty, nasty bully
G rumpy, guilty bully.

Jonathon Walsh (11)
Rough Hay Primary School

Trouble With A Dinosaur

There was a visitor at the door
It was a hungry dinosaur
I gave him onion soup with crusty bread
He preferred the furniture instead
He roared and he stomped and he bothered me all day
So I didn't get to go out and play
When Mom came home her face turned pink
The dinosaur was splashing in the sink
I don't mind people stopping for tea
But a dinosaur is much too big for me.

Toni-Ann Keise (8)
SS Mary & John's RC Primary School

At School

When I went to school today my teacher had gone mad,
She said when I was being good, that I was being bad.
And when we were meant to be doing RE
The teacher started doing karate!
When it was home time at five-past three
The teacher dressed up as a bumblebee
And flew out the school gate!

Isobel Barrett (9)
SS Mary & John's RC Primary School

My Auntie Shirley

I had a strange auntie called Shirley
Whose hair was incredibly curly.
She looked like a poodle,
Each hair was a noodle
Extremely twisty and twirly.

Iona Gulyas (9)
SS Mary & John's RC Primary School

Grandad

Grandad you were to me
Everything a dad could be
When in trouble to you I came
Through the snow, sun and the rain
You used to sit me on your knee
And talk about the apple tree
Now you're gone I'm all alone
No more talking on the phone
Grandad why did you leave me here to stay?

Sinitta Banga (9)
SS Mary & John's RC Primary School

Plants

Plants, plants, they're very nice they are just like spice.
Sometimes yellow, sometimes green, sometimes tall and lean.
I like tulips and I like roses
I like daisies and also posies.
They smell fresh and nice too
And I would like to smell them instead of my shoe!

Cherise Dixon (7)
SS Mary & John's RC Primary School

My Best Friend

My pencil is my best friend; we will always be together.
My pencil is my best friend, whatever the weather.
To talk to my pencil I don't need a phone,
When I've got my pencil I'm never alone.
My pencil tells me stories; it plays games with me,
My pencil tells me all about maths and geography.

Manraaj Saini (9)
SS Mary & John's RC Primary School

Tiger

Silent hunter
Big pouncer
Tree climber
Prey killer
Brave fighter
Good sighter
Scary caller
Loud roarer
Fast runner
A stunner!

Heather Stark (9)
SS Mary & John's RC Primary School

My Mom

Love giver
Hug sharer
Quick talker
Best speller
Good cooker
Kind teacher
Friendly carer
Potato peeler!

Jake Smith (8)
SS Mary & John's RC Primary School

Butterfly

Peaceful and calm
Like a charm
You flow like the wind
You glorious thing.

Selina Peake (9)
SS Mary & John's RC Primary School

Miss Lester-Teacher

Chocolate lover
Loud shouter
Careful listener
Deep thinker
Happy teacher
Hard worker
Fun teacher
Quiet whisper
It's Miss Lester.

Callam Cartwright (8)
SS Mary & John's RC Primary School

Great White Shark

Flesh ripper
Leg eater
Blood lover
Non storer
Human hater
False mover
Bone breaker
Paralyse maker.

Christian McNulty (9)
SS Mary & John's RC Primary School

Mrs Bagga

Hard worker
Great thinker
Friendly helper
Fun teacher.

Audrey Murambiwa (9)
SS Mary & John's RC Primary School

My Mom

'Get me my bag!'
'Make me something to eat!'
'I won't like you bowling!'
'I'll get you a treat!'
'Pick your brother up!'
'Open the door to your dad!'
'Go on . . . '
'I'm going.' (slam!)

Inderpreet Uppal (8)
SS Mary & John's RC Primary School

Who Am I?

I am a quiet hunter,
Fast runner
Loud caller
Great climber
Hard eater
Wild fighter
Who am I?

A: jaguar.

Ashley Raju (9)
SS Mary & John's RC Primary School

Monkey

A banana lover
A good hugger
A cheeky soul
Full of laughter.

Rebecca Marshall (8)
SS Mary & John's RC Primary School